Someone Destroyed My Rocket Ship

and other havoc I've witnessed at the office

Copyright © 2018 Dushka Zapata

All rights reserved

ISBN: 1719023123

ISBN-13: 978-1719023122

My dear, find what you love and let it kill you.

Let it drain you of your all.

Let it cling onto your back and weigh you down into eventual nothingness.

Let it kill you and let it devour your remains.

For all things will kill you, both slowly and fastly, but it's much better to be killed by a lover.

— **Charles Bukowski**

For Analisa.

Contents

But First, You	1
Communication	53
How to Thrive as an Introvert	77
Your Resume and How to Interview	95
Your First Job	121
Media and Presentation Training	145
Am I Doing This Right?	169
Who am I?	227
Leaving Your Job	273
Starting Over	291

But First, You

*Until you make the unconscious conscious,
it will direct your life and you will call it fate.*

— Carl Jung

What I Owe Myself

I owe it to myself to assume others have good intentions and are trying their best. It's better to travel through life unburdened by suspicion, better to be disappointed sometimes than to be encumbered always.

I owe it to myself to banish blame. I prefer to be accountable for who I am and what I do. I prefer to be powerful.

I owe it to myself to imagine the best-case scenario instead of the worst-case scenario. They are equally plausible and when the worst does happen it only hurts one time, instead of the recurring blows inherent in fervent anticipation.

I owe it to myself to interpret the story of my life in a way that casts me as fortunate.

I owe it to myself to learn to ignore my inner voice any time it tells me I can't do something. The world imposes enough limits on me. I don't need to contribute against myself.

I owe it to myself to remember that the difference between an adventure (exciting), and an obstacle (frustrating) is how I choose to regard it.

I owe it to myself to identify what I don't like within me and dedicate all the resources available to me to address them.

I owe it to myself to love and admire the people closest to me. We become so much of what we surround ourselves with.

I owe it to myself to find cruelty unacceptable.

If a series of conclusions can all be equally true, I owe it to myself to choose the option that makes me suffer the least. To suggest to myself that "he never really loved me" is absurd, and needlessly painful.

I owe it to myself to believe in luck, in miracles and in magic. I owe it to myself to believe in absurdly frequent serendipity. I owe it to myself to believe that anything can happen.

I owe it to myself to see that I am always learning something new.

I owe it to myself to not believe everything I think.

The Worst Kind Of Procrastination

My father had an incredible life.

By "incredible" I mean that if I told you about it you'd have trouble believing me.

My father dined with kings. He represented my country. He had many wives; I don't know how many lovers.

Through his entire life he counted on some day writing his autobiography.

This is how he would spend his "golden years". Writing about his life adventures.

Except he developed dementia.

He was startlingly intelligent, ridiculously funny, the best storyteller of all time and loved to write.

My heart is irreparably crushed by the loss of this book that was never written.

There are two types of procrastination.

The one where you leave for later something you don't want to do.

The second type of procrastination is more insidious and more difficult to recognize.

It's when you leave for later the things you want to do the most.

This requires that you disguise procrastination with responsibility.

I really want to write a book but first I need to clean the house.

Then, I will do laundry.

Then, I will go to work. I have to pay the bills.

This is how your book is never written.

Never postpone what makes you feel fulfilled.

Don't let the book of your life remain unwritten.

Proud Of Me

One morning many years ago, my Dad, my two younger brothers and I were having breakfast.

"Some day," my father told one of my brothers, *"you will be a doctor."*

"What about me?" said the other.

"You," my Dad said with a smile *"will be a lawyer."*

"And me?" I asked.

"You," he said anointing me, *"you are going to be the mother of my grandchildren."*

I imagine this conversation, taken out of context and out of time, would spark outrage. But my father loved me. This was his dream.

Back then, his words filled my chest. Someday my children would run in his garden and sit with him in his library.

Except, that never happened. I went to work and loved it: the challenge, the discipline, the variety, the demands. I got married quite young and got a divorce less than a year later.

If I could summarize the trajectory of life I'd say that things do not turn out the way you plan them, and that this is the best part.

It's where the astonishment is, the awe and the gratitude.

Along the rocky way you will disappoint so many people, in particular the people who love you the most, including yourself. This is the mark of a life that belongs only to you.

Despite any temporary delusion, the fact is you are never obligated to do anything you might believe you are supposed to do.

You possess the greatest gift bestowed on humankind: free will.

You can but don't have to find a significant other, a house, have a wedding, have children. These are all options that work for a few people but not for others.

(Anecdotally, I had a wonderful significant other and a beautiful house and a loving wedding only to realize I wasn't happy and wanted none of it.)

In one of the great paradoxes of life, no matter what you do everyone will judge you and nobody will care.

For both of these reasons what others think about your choices should not be given much consideration.

I buried my father three years ago. I never gave him any of the things he wanted for me.

I can tell you without a doubt that for everything I am and everything I have done, for every choice I made, every mistake, every flaw, every shortcoming, he was incalculably, inestimably, recklessly proud of me.

How To Accelerate Your Personal Growth

Own your trajectory. There are things — such as motivation, a challenge, and work/life balance — that we tend to put in the hands of others. Let me save you time: no one will do this for you.

Divorce yourself from the thought that you deserve something. Entitlement breeds mediocrity.

Conversely, get over yourself. I often don't ask for what I want because I feel I should get it without having to ask. This is preposterous. Just ask.

Self-promotion is very hard for many of us. Turn it on its head. Is anything that you are doing useful to others? Share it. Tell others how you arrived at it.

Make things simple, the reverse of pretension and big words makes others feel clear-headed rather than inadequate.

Trying to get something perfect is your archenemy, not your goal.

Deliver on what you promise. Never underestimate the power of being the one people can count on.

Develop a point of view. Find your voice.

As my friend Christopher Lochhead says *"**position yourself or be positioned**"*. Figure out who you are and what you can offer to find what makes you different. If you are better, you are competing. If you are different no one can do what you do.

If you could find a person who could consistently lighten your load with solid, unique insight, wouldn't that make your day better? This can only mean one thing: **everyone around you is waiting for you to tell them what to do.**

Every day, step back to regard the big picture. How does everything connect? And what might it mean? Learn how to recognize trends. This is visionary training.

Learn how to work with others. Play well with others. Help others up.

Trust the people you work with. Forget about them being or not being trustworthy. You don't have the energy to go through life being suspicious of everyone. You have other things to focus on.

No matter what they say at your next performance review, disregard the absurd notion of "improving on your weaknesses". **Focus on your strengths instead.** By the way, realize your strengths and weaknesses are the same thing. Eradicate one, affect the other.

Do less. Operating as if you never have enough time, not getting enough sleep, burning the candle at both ends will result in burnout, not success. Failure is necessary. The opposite of success is burnout.

Do what you love. This is not the rosy, fluffy advice of an incorrigible dreamer (which I most certainly am). If you are slogging through something you cannot compete with someone who can't get enough of it.

Optimism Is Good For You

If you believe something is not possible, that something is out of your reach, you will look for confirmation that what you believe is true.

Your brain is trying to defend what it thinks, so proof of the opposite of what it thinks will be discarded.

In other words, your brain actively deletes any alternative because it wants to confirm that whatever you believe in is true.

For example, I used to believe that I couldn't afford to resign from my job.

This belief was Truth to me and I argued to defend it.

I actually defended something that made me feel trapped and anxious.

The day I decided to resign my reality changed. I wanted quitting to be viable and every day a new path opened before me.

A path that had been there all along.

It's not that the universe unfolds before me in a way that makes my life easier to live because it loves me (although it certainly feels that way). It's that your perspective is different: it's open to options.

You always have choices. You often, without knowing that you are doing so, refuse to see them.

Your attitude gives your brain instructions on what to see.

This is why it's important to come at things from a place of receptivity and peace rather than from a place of stress. *"What is it that I am not seeing?"* is so much better than *"OH MY GOD THERE IS NO WAY OUT"*.

You cannot be too optimistic, unless you think you can.

In which case you will prove to yourself that you are right.

Productivity And Efficiency

An appliance is infallibly efficient. A machine is relentlessly productive.

I'm not an automaton. If efficiency and productivity were the focal points of my day, my soul would starve.

I need down time, idle time, relaxed time, unstructured time. Without it my creativity suffers, my insight, but also a fundamental sense of perspective, which is precisely what makes me valuable at work.

And, what about the things I consider most important, the people that I love?

Is spending a Sunday coloring with my niece and nephew efficient? Is going to the movies with friends productive? Is pressing the snooze button so I can snuggle a bit longer an ideal way to manage my time?

Probably not. But, what could be more important than that?

On days of maximum productivity I don't look up at the sky to witness the fog rolling in. I don't stop to ask my friend at work what she did over the weekend. I don't savor my food or even realize I'm thirsty. I don't feel the wind mess with my hair as I dash out of the office to catch my bus.

I can assure you that nothing I produce ever matters more than the time I spend producing nothing.

Does Luck Play Any Role In Success?

I almost wish I could deny the existence of luck. Without it I'd be able to take full credit for my astoundingly blessed life.

I don't deserve full credit. I don't know where I'd be without sheer, pure, unadulterated good fortune.

I find it indispensable and can only hope it keeps striking me as it has.

In exchange, I will continue to be both deeply grateful and filled with wonder.

Personality Tests

What if we found a reliable way to slot humans into categories to make relationships easier and more productive?

How alluring.

How dangerous.

But mostly, how preposterous.

We are incredibly complicated and unpredictable. We're not binary. We can be one thing one day and another thing an hour later. (Or maybe that's just me.)

We cannot really be "managed for efficiency".

We can't even manage ourselves for efficiency.

I'm sorry to be the one to tell you that what we are is a glorious mess.

Personality tests attempt to fit us neatly into largely arbitrary, unscientific categories. Every category is described predominantly with positive words and is therefore extra tempting.

But most people don't really fall into one letter or its opposite. They fall somewhere in between. Or manage to be both.

I can (and do) both think and feel at the same time.

Whenever a company I work for offers a personality test I ask myself *"even if it's not viable to define me (or anyone), what can I take from this that would serve me?"*

A personality test revealed to me that I recharge by being alone, which has proven astoundingly useful.

That being said, I also love talking to strangers.

Putting ourselves into a category is delicious. The feeling of *YES OH MY GOD THAT IS TOTALLY ME* makes us feel deeply understood.

As tempting as it is, though, personality tests are not a reliable path to understanding ourselves better.

I wish it was that easy.

The Gift Of Silence

The world is such a noisy place. To that I add the rattling in my head: to do lists and where I have to go and be and how I'm going to get there and what time.

Find a few minutes a day — even five, but more if possible — and find your seat.

Let the dust settle around you.

Listen to your breath.

Set aside everything that worries or burdens you, just for those few minutes.

I promise it will all be there for you to pick up when you're done.

It doesn't matter where you sit or if you are sitting on the floor or in what position.

It doesn't matter if you can't stop your thoughts (no one can).

All that matters is that you give yourself a corner, an edge, a taste, a sip of silence.

That you take a few minutes to notice and appreciate your own breath and how it flows in and out.

In and out.

Sometimes I put a hand on my chest and feel the beating of my heart and focus on that.

That works too.

Come back for more any time.

How To Get In Your Own Way

Develop a tendency to take everything personally. Be hurt and defensive any time anyone provides feedback.

Remind yourself that your way is the only way. Interfere with people's work, then determine to redo it yourself for it to "get done right".

Dislike someone. Intensely. Gossip about them. Gossip about everyone.

Worry. Extra points if fretting keeps you up at night.

Hold indignant imaginary conversations where you predict another person's reaction. Go through every possible scenario.

Assume that things that appear to be larger than you are actually about you.

Hold meetings with unclear objectives.

When you're feeling paranoid, analyze every unrelated event until it all resembles evidence that the world is indeed out to get you.

Complain. Make sure you make the complaints elliptical by finding people who have similar issues so that beyond discussing them over and over no action to resolve them is ever taken.

Assume it is someone else's job to solve the problems you feel hindered by.

Anticipate the worst-case scenario so you can feel stressed about outcomes that are not likely to happen.

Instead of learning new things, engage and amplify office politics so that on the off-chance they play a role in you being successful in your current job they render you unsuitable for anything that comes after.

What Makes Me Tense

I frequently feel like I can't take my time. Like I have to handle multiple things at once, make to do lists and check items off, struggle to remain organized, keep on top of it all.

If only I could breathe.

Taking time off work would help for sure. Working in a fast paced, demanding industry that requires juggling, multitasking and handling conflicting priorities was clearly to blame.

I quit my job for many reasons but one of them was this desperate, bone-deep yearning for *time.*

As I began my new life of temporary unemployment I set goals for myself, things I wanted to accomplish while I was off work.

Very quickly I found myself back to feeling I had no time. Like I had to handle multiple things at once, make to do lists and check items off, struggle to remain organized, keep on top of it all.

We blame the outside for things that are really happening inside.

It's me.

I make me tense.

Distraction

I could make a list as long as my arm of little things that annoy me.

Just today, lukewarm coffee and formatting issues and interruptions.

But, you know what? When a little thing annoys me, if I stop and ask myself *"OK. What is really going on here?"* there is always a big thing.

Little things are a diversion. They are a distraction. See the big thing for what it is so you can name it and address it.

Then you won't even notice the little things that once annoyed you.

Bitch

When I was a little girl my brothers were told they were brave. I was told I would need protecting. For them, I heard words like "strong", "solid", "big". For me, "sweet", "adorable", "pretty". What I strived for was to be a good girl. I still do.

Later, in school, boys were encouraged to act with courage, vigor, conviction. I needed to be more careful with my passions, lest I come across as dramatic or emotional. A man was persistent. I was a nag. A man was the boss, I was bossy, pushy.

I've been called a "bitch" for holding my ground or for saying no to sexual advances. I've been called a slut for saying yes and for liking sex as much as you.

I am frequently told I am not like other women, like this is supposed to be a huge compliment. I aspire to be like so many women I know.

I am assertive and unfailingly have an opinion. Recently, in a meeting, I confessed to a (female) friend and co-worker that I am perpetually worried about coming on too strong. I spend a lot of my energy pulling back, worried I am talking too much. *"Dushka,"* she said, *"I have never, ever heard a man worry about something like that."*

I have been working in communications and PR in the tech industry for over 20 years. I have spent that same amount of time listening to men who have never worked in public relations patiently explain to me how I should be doing my job.

It's hard to be a strong woman. It's hard to have a strong personality and to see people feel threatened by the fact you disagree.

Over the years I have been setting down so many expectations I had put on myself. I have for years worked full time and insisted on assuming responsibility for anything to do with organizing, coordinating, cleaning, shopping, socializing. I don't do that anymore. I don't cook, and that's a fact, not a shortcoming.

I like who I am so much and look at other strong women and want them to like who they are too. I trust them. I tell them I find them intelligent, even when they are wearing awesome shoes. I remind myself to recognize their work when I introduce them. I make room for them to feel comfortable speaking up in meetings. I both promote and recruit them.

If they have an opinion they are expressing with vigor, with conviction, with passion, I wholeheartedly support them, and regardless of your gender, so should you.

What Is "Stubborn"?

I am frequently considered "stubborn".

In particular when I was a little girl, adults would encourage me to do something in a specific way.

I realized later that I don't learn by being told or dictated. I learn by figuring it out. I'm not being stubborn deliberately — I'm trying to understand it.

Throughout my life I have found that when someone accuses me of being stubborn, it's because I want to listen to myself instead of listening to them.

It sounds like a version of this: *Why do you want to do what you want instead of what I want?*

To riff off of Ambrose Bierce's *The Devil's Dictionary*, I would define stubborn as *"a selfish person who insists on doing things their way instead of mine."*

Ordinary Hero

How often do you feel you need more sleep when the alarm goes off? You get up and get on with your day despite fatigue.

How many times do you resist lashing out at someone, hold in your frustration, your anger? How frequently do you make an effort to, rather than snap, react instead with compassion?

Have you felt you just want to be a better friend, a better parent, a better family member, a better spouse?

You do well one day and not so well another but marshal your forces and return to battle the next day.

How many times are you generous when no one is watching?

How many times do you emerge victorious from internal battles no one else can see?

I really admire big, flashy, single acts of heroism; but I also recognize the effort of rising to the occasion day in, day out.

The "every day" is relentless. It requires so much work.

Without diminishing the traditional definition of a hero, let's recognize the small, ordinary hero inside each of us, the one who shows up every day.

The Person Playing Tricks On You Is You

I set the alarm for 5:45 to make it to an early morning yoga class. It clears my head, and my head needs clearing.

The alarm goes off.

Skip the class, my brain says. *Go back to sleep.*

But —

Sleep is important. Catch another hour or two and go to a later class. You usually go in the evening anyway.

But —

It's dark out. And chilly. It's so warm in here. You've been to yoga every day this week. Even if you skip this class it won't matter. It won't make a difference.

I grab my phone and turn off the alarm (instead of touching that ever evil snooze button).

I get up.

Because, my mind plays tricks on me every day, but, you know what?

She is not the boss of me.

Be The One Who Can't Do That

A friend recently hurt his lower back and I suggested he attend a few yoga classes as part of his physical therapy. He shook his head. *"I don't want to be that guy."*

Huh?

"You know. The old guy. The stiff guy. The fat guy. The guy who can't do what everyone is doing."

I told him that the whole point of yoga is that it's for everybody, and that part of what it teaches you is about accepting where you are at, rather than falling into the habit of constantly comparing yourself to others.

Then I confessed that as dismayed as I was by his answer, the truth was I could relate.

How many times have I stopped myself from asking a question for fear it will make me look ignorant? How many times have I refrained from participating in something lest it make me look incapable or incompetent?

I am impressed by anyone who shoves aside the universal *"Oh, no, how is this going to make me look!?"* to make courageous, glorious room to learn something new or welcome a fresh experience.

That's the kind of spirit that inspires me to set aside any absurd concern for something as trivial as appearances and instead be open to making a true and complete fool out of myself.

Strength/Weakness

Thinking about your strengths and weaknesses as separate affects your ability to understand yourself.

You strengths and your weaknesses are one and the same.

Here is an example.

I recently worked with a wonderful, intelligent, ambitious woman who found she was having trouble getting ahead.

She was involved, driven, action oriented and open to feedback. The type of person who "gets things done".

If our strengths are also our weaknesses, can we take a look at the price her motivation comes with?

What are the disadvantages of a singular focus on getting things done?

She is always managing high levels of stress. I encourage her to take a breath, to intentionally let some time go by (sometimes an extra minute, sometimes a night) between a thought and her reaction to the thought.

This, compounded, will result in less anxiety, less mental frenzy, added clarity and focus; also in action that is more deliberate and thought through.

I suggest she take the time to read others. If her focus is getting things done, she is thinking of what to say or do while the other person (often her manager) is still talking.

Can we listen without any other intent? If we cannot, what are we missing?

What about collaboration? Action oriented people have a tendency to be faster, more efficient than others, and as such often resolve to act alone. *"This will be easier if I just get it done."*

But, this often means we sacrifice what we might learn from others.

Collaboration might compromise speed and might not come naturally, but it arrives with other benefits, one of which is increased self-awareness.

The same applies to our ability to delegate. *"For this to get done right, I have to do it"* is the sign of a bad manager. It means we impair others and affect our own ability to scale.

Delegation means growth: for others and for ourselves.

The most important thing we can learn from this strength/weakness perspective is that it's not supposed to be this hard.

Feeling like we need to react quickly, like there is no time, like we can't take a second to assess what another is going through, like everything has to get done by me and only me, is exhausting, isolating, unsustainable.

Learning more about ourselves is about suffering less.

What Motivates You?

I'm in the kitchen, surveying the refrigerator and pulling things out.

I begin chopping various vegetables.

I will create oven-roasted something.

Based on prior experiences I can say that what I make is likely to be good and unlikely to be epic.

If Boyfriend were here and in my same situation — standing in the kitchen, surveying the refrigerator, planning on cooking something — the chances that he'd come up with a memorable concoction are at about 99%.

You see, when Boyfriend cooks, his motivation is *"I want to make something delicious!"*

When I cook, my motivation is *"I want to clean out the refrigerator!"*

What motivates you?

Most of the complex answers we look for can be found within simple, everyday things.

When Making A Decision, What Kind Of Thinking Is Not A Part Of Your Ego?

Imagine for a moment that I am in a company meeting. Many important people are sitting around the table.

I want to say something.

Wait. Let's take a look.

Do I want to say something because I want to be seen, to be heard, because I want people to think highly of me and witness me in all my mastery, glory and prowess?

That's my ego.

Do I want to say something because I have insight that is clarifying, useful, helpful or valuable?

That's me.

I try not to let my ego make my decisions.

How To Practice Being Secure

Listen to yourself and make your own decisions. Ask for advice but ultimately realize your best guide is you, even if what you think you should do goes against what everyone is telling you. Even your best friend. Even your parents.

Walk away from gossip. Talking about others or listening to people talk about others is time you could be spending on your own shortcomings.

Speak up. Even at the risk of being wrong.

Don't try to please everyone. Living your life pleasing others compromises your perspective and your priorities. Plus, it is a futile undertaking. It can't be done.

Listen and be grateful for feedback.

Accept compliments.

Stop worrying about being wrong, failing or not doing something perfectly. You're not perfect. Everyone already knows.

Try new things. New things are fun even though you will probably be very bad at them, at least in the beginning. Being very bad at something is good for the soul.

Pull other people up. If you learn something that was valuable to you, share it. If there is something you can do to make the path easier for another, do it. Because another person's gain is your gain.

Surround yourself with people who are better than you. Be in awe of your friends and coworkers, welcome different perspectives.

Ask for help even if this reveals you actually do need others.

How Do I Stay In The Present?

To stay present you anchor your thoughts and sensations in whatever is happening right now.

Take deep breaths. Notice your breath and where it goes in the body, how it flows in and out, what parts of you are expanding or contracting.

Tune in. What can you hear? I am on a plane and can hear the whirring engine, the shrieks of a small child, unintelligible conversations.

What can you see? I can see the wall in front of me, the airplane carpet, people sitting around me, the boy sitting next to me playing a game on his iPad.

How do you feel? My shoulders are tight, and I'm a bit chilly. I can feel the weight of the seatbelt on my lap. My eyes burn a bit due to the dry airplane air.

This exercise grounds me. I feel less angst when I focus on now rather than running a to do list in my brain of all the things I need to do after I land.

I sometimes feel like to do lists soothe me but it's a trap.

When I run a to do list in my brain it wants more.

What am I forgetting? Should I go over it again?

I will always have things to add to this list. It is insatiable.

What If I'm Wrong?

My brain was designed to assess a situation and make a quick decision. To execute on this, I call upon my gut, my instinct. The resulting conclusion is the beginning of what I will soon hold as truth.

Once I hold this truth, facts are scary if they go against what my brain arrived at.

If I feel one thing and a fact indicates another, then this means I might be (gasp) wrong.

If I can't believe what I think, what is left for me to believe?

In order to survive this predicament, I make the choice of disbelieving the fact because the alternative would be to question myself. If I can't believe myself, I have nothing to stand on.

To stay safe, to tether myself to the notion that I can believe in myself, I don't only dismiss the fact, but I proceed to look for any evidence that confirms what I already believe. I use selective facts and then use them to rationalize my initial conclusion.

It takes real presence of mind to recognize that a fact that proves me wrong does not really threaten me. That I can survive being wrong many times, and can use facts to learn.

Reality is better than considering that something is real because I feel it is.

Insecurity Is A Universal Condition

A prestigious, well known company recently hired me to train a six person team on how to come across in a stronger, more compelling way.

As part of the assignment I spent a few days looking at videos of them presenting at conferences and events.

They were really, really good.

On the night before their session I had trouble sleeping. I was concerned they were already so competent I would have nothing of value to add.

The next day I went into the conference room they were all in and introduced myself. Then I presented my agenda for the next three hours and asked if what I intended to do was aligned with their expectations.

A woman raised her hand.

"Dushka, I am so nervous. I think we are all feeling somewhat intimidated."

It really helps to know that while you might feel alone in your insecurities every one of them is a universal condition.

Help Yourself

Scenario one:

Imagine that today you have an important meeting first thing in the morning.

You are afraid that you will not do well which resulted in a restless night.

You set the alarm and hit the snooze button and overslept and now you are running late. You are stressed.

You arrive at the meeting frazzled and unprepared.

Scenario two:

Imagine that today you have an important meeting first thing in the morning.

You are afraid you will not do well, and take the necessary time to talk yourself through this fear and how irrational it is.

In part you are afraid because you constantly practice self-criticism and self-doubt. Instead, practice telling yourself there is a reason why you are running this meeting.

What else? Are there parts of the meeting that particularly worry you? Could that concern be reduced by being more diligent about preparing?

Can you develop intelligent answers to the questions you are most afraid of?

You make it a point to go to bed extra early so you are well rested.

You set the alarm a full hour before you really need to, in an attempt to give yourself the soothing luxury of extra time.

You meditate, sip coffee peacefully, pick out an outfit that is appropriate and comfortable, read through your notes, rehearse.

You might walk into the meeting feeling nervous, but you are pulled together. You've got this.

There is a nearly infinite amount of things that you have control over that steal your power away from you.

Think through what they are and get out in front of them instead.

Someone Destroyed My Rocket Ship

Six year old nephew: *"ACK ACK SOMEONE DESTROYED MY ROCKET SHIP WHY WHY WOULD SOMEONE DO THIS ACK!"*

Me: *"Remember when you stacked all the cushions to make the pillow fort and the cushion pushed your rocket ship off the shelf?"*

Him: *"Yeah."*

Me: *"Who destroyed the rocket ship?"*

Him: *"The cushion."*

Me: *"Who was the mastermind behind the cushion?"*

Him: *"Me."*

Me: *"So, who are you mad at?"*

Him: *"Me."*

He nods bravely.

Accountability is the opposite of blame, and it is awesome.

It Comes From You

I have collaborated with absolutely calm CEOs who are working through a crisis situation that has the potential to obliterate their company.

I have also worked with individuals who have money and have decided to take time off and don't know what to do next and are freaking out.

Stress does not come from the job. It comes from you.

Don't Think

I come from an intellectual family. Whenever I didn't know what to do or I did something wrong my Dad would say *"Dushka, think."* It wasn't until much later in life that I was instructed to "get out of my head and into my body".

"Don't think" seemed preposterous to me. Reason was supposed to override everything.

I have since learned that my thoughts are chatter and often suggest contradictory things. They don't decide. I do. My thoughts are only suggestions and many of them come from my insecurities (I definitely don't want to listen to those).

The master is me.

To distinguish who is who, I need to sit in silence and listen to my breath. My noisy brain will never stop thinking. Thinking is what it does. But focusing on my breath allows me to sift through who is thinking all these thoughts.

If I sit in silence for a couple of minutes, breathe, and sleep on important decisions, my brain sorts things out without my intervention. I don't need to understand how this happens. There is no instruction manual to follow. I don't need to do anything other than listen to myself through focusing on my breath for a few minutes.

"Don't think. Breathe." didn't make sense to me, but when it did it shifted my priorities. It quiets down my rowdy monkey brain. It taught me to listen to myself.

Unrequited Feelings Towards A Coworker

Any and all the unrequited love I feel is my responsibility.

If I love someone who doesn't feel the same way, what feels beautiful to me feels invasive to him.

What feels like an offering to me is an imposition to him.

What feels uplifting to me feels encroaching to him.

What feels like massive restraint to me is (hopefully) undetectable (or maybe awkward) to him.

He is not responsible for how I feel. He is not obligated to do anything about this frankly off-kilter other person.

I don't want to take something buoyant and turn myself into a nuisance. I need to contain this, manage this, own this, or take myself somewhere else with this.

I need to put an end to this. It makes me sad, but what feels sad to me feels like relief to him.

I cannot burden another with my brimming, spilling, sparking feelings. They are mine.

A List Worth Making

A friend of mine attended a workshop to learn how to better prioritize.

The person leading the workshop asked the participants to begin by taking stock of their lives.

As a first step they had to make a list of all the things they were not happy with.

(If you'd like to try this exercise stop here and make this list before you read until the end. It's worth it, I promise.)

My friend's list looked something like this:

I never take my kids to school because my day begins too early.

I don't talk to my wife all day because I'm booked with meetings and don't have time to call.

I never get home in time to put my kids to bed.

I work every weekend.

I feel disconnected from my family.

Once the participants finished making their lists they were asked to read them out loud.

Except, they needed to begin each sentence with *"I am committed to..."*.

For example: I am committed to never taking my kids to school.

When my friend read his list out loud he had a startling realization.

That what he was saying sounded absolutely absurd, and that, incredibly, this was exactly what he was doing: dedicating himself to all the things that were making him unhappy.

This exercise drove the message home that where we spend our time reveals our true priorities and that we have a choice to determine what to be committed to.

Is Diversity A Good Thing?

The term "diversity" refers to the act of including in an endeavor individuals from different orientations, colors, religions or origin.

In the interest of a comprehensive answer I need to begin by explaining there is an inherent bias in asking it.

The question betrays you have never felt excluded or mistreated because of where you are from, your color, your religion or your sexual preference.

People who have find this question offensive, even hurtful.

The better we can see how we are perceived and the effect what we say and do has on others the better we can connect to the world around us.

Do you know what is essential to improving self-awareness?

Diversity.

Diversity is a good thing because we should foster an environment that feels like everyone belongs and is respected.

My perception of the world is not reality. It's just my perception. If I am to inch closer to the way things actually are I need to add the perception of others. Diversity is a good thing because it's the way to understand the world.

An environment that is diverse is essential even in managing the constant stress caused by my own distorted imagination. Operating in such an environment invites me to plug in, get out of the limited confines of my head and become gloriously aware of the existence, the needs, the feelings and the vantage point of humans who are different than me.

Without diversity I would first impair, then atrophy my ability to negotiate, relate, teach, learn, persuade, sell, convince, influence or be a true team player.

Every time you declare a problem unsolvable someone who does not think like you can see clear as day a solution you cannot.

The opposite of diversity is not uniformity. It's ignorance. And that's why it's essential.

Game Changer

I am frequently a part of conversations regarding *"who we need to hire".*

Most leaders I know want the same thing.

Someone to come in *with fresh eyes. A new perspective.* A person who *does things differently.* Who can *take things to the next level.*

Everybody wants *a game changer.*

Then, once the person has started, it's better if they are more like everyone else. *It's not good to rock the boat. Processes should be respected.*

Because, that's not how things are done here.

We hire people because they are different, and then we want them all to be the same.

We need to have the courage to stick with what we want.

Employees can absolutely succeed in the workplace, even when they are not a natural cultural fit.

Because the best workplaces celebrate misfits.

This is the true meaning of cultural diversity.

The Youngest Person In The Room

For many years I struggled with the fact that in every meeting I was the youngest person in the room.

It was my job to advise communications teams what to say to external audiences; suggest to executives what to tell press, how to structure an answer for the media, and what to do during a time of crisis.

What they saw when I walked in was a kid.

This sense of being the youngest person in the room, and with it an imperative to overcompensate, over-prepare and present strong arguments for every little thing, stayed with me long after I was no longer the youngest person in the room.

I have no idea exactly when that happened.

One day a client going through a crisis told me they needed their communications team to be led by a professional with years of experience who could be involved every day on site to help them navigate the months of delicate decisions that awaited them.

I said I would make sure someone with those qualifications was added to the team. They looked at me strangely.

"No, Dushka. We mean we want you."

Communication

The single biggest problem in communication is the illusion that it has taken place.

— George Bernard Shaw

We Are All Different

I once hired a woman who did brilliant work but was not a good team player. It's not that she was destructive or hostile. It was more that, in an industry that typically thrives on collaboration, she was an independent contributor.

Another employee was always late. I felt it reflected a lack of interest and discipline but he consistently delivered high quality work.

Another had to leave early, every day, no exceptions, and was never available or reachable outside of traditional office hours. Public Relations, the industry I have worked in all my life, is not a 9:00 to 5:00 job. It often requires people stay late. If someone always leaves early it puts the burden on other team members.

Another employee was terrified of doing a presentation, another was not a good writer, another was easily stressed and tended to regard everything as a crisis.

All of these employees were excellent in other aspects of the job, but these characteristics, I thought, were "essential".

As a manager, for years I strived to "correct" this kind of behavior. I tried to get the independent contributor to become a team player, to get everyone to show up on time, to encourage a bit of flexibility in the person who was never available after hours.

I tried to work on people's "shortcomings" instead of playing to their strengths.

Then I realized that what I was doing was trying to make everyone the same in an environment that thrived on everyone being different.

That there was no such thing as someone who was good at everything.

That the best thing I could do as a manager was find the right place for an employee, where who the person already was would contribute to making the operation as a whole successful.

If you interview high level executives — such as CEOs — and ask them what keeps them up at night, the consistent reply is "talent".

People who deliver brilliant work are hard to come by.

It's our job as managers to make our business environment flexible enough to give every brilliant employee a place to thrive.

Small Talk

Small talk is not conversation. It's a social lubricant.

What you are really saying is: *Hi! I'm friendly and harmless and I want you to like me!*

To which the other person responds: *What a tremendous coincidence! What are the chances!? I too am friendly and harmless and would love it if you liked me!*

Small talk is a social skill and intended as a way to open the conversation and transition on to more meaningful things. You are putting a toe in the water before jumping into the deep end with a person you have not fully identified.

I have witnessed small talk artists in action and can tell you that done well it's like a dance. It's light and effervescent and everyone is put at ease and smiling.

I am atrocious at small talk, which is likely to be one of the reasons I hate it so much. I find it inane, inauthentic and mind-numbingly boring. I tend to either mumble, back away or blurt out something intense or personal (to which my small talk artist friend sighs and says *"Oh, Dushka. I can't take you anywhere."*).

Connect

When I was growing up (many years ago but also yesterday) and met someone my first thought was *"I want you to think highly of me."*

I wanted the other person to think I was awesome so spent time and energy attempting to be unbelievably impressive.

This was less about *"I am the best"*, and more about *"please, please like me"*.

And yet, do you know how the other person felt?

You are not listening. You are all about yourself. I have been trying to tell you something and you keep interrupting.

This is because the other person didn't give a hoot how glorious my achievements were. She (or he) had her own needs.

Can you guess what they were?

She wanted me to think highly of her.

This wasn't about her insisting *"I am the best"*, but more about her wishing I would like her.

So there we were. I spun stories and used all my favorite words, an ocean of flashy words, and she made grand, swinging gestures and each of us, wrapped up in our demands, were too occupied to ever make the connection we both craved.

So I put it all down. I try my best (with varying levels of success) to meet people empty handed, completely open to what they want to tell me or show me, and all I give them in return is me.

To Be Clear

To communicate with clarity, here is a list of things I stop doing:

I stop using my powers for evil. If my words are not aligned with positive intent things tend to end up a chaotic mess.

I try to use words for love, for truth, for constructive endeavors.

I discard spite, revenge, gossip, manipulation.

It's not that I'm pure and virtuous. It's that I've learned the hard way it doesn't end well.

I stop speaking before understanding what I want. How can I be clear about anything if I don't know what it is?

I stop lying. If I lie, then I lie to cover the lie. Then it's hard to trust me, and for a long time nothing is clear. Nothing.

I stop confusing the goal. Instead of the objective "communicate clearly" I want to win the argument or arrive at a specific outcome. Winning and any form of manipulation arrest clear communication.

I stop believing I have extrasensory perception. Nothing causes more drama and confusion than assuming, guessing, or believing I can read someone's mind. Expecting anyone can read mine is equally catastrophic.

I stop throwing in too many messages. The more I try to say the less clearly I am understood and the less memorable what I say becomes.

The clearer my communication, the cleaner my life becomes.

Texting

Texting can be an excellent form of communication if what you need to say is clear cut.

"I will be home at 8:00."

"We're out of milk. Can you get some?"

Texting can be terrible if the situation is emotional, if you know you should be doing this in person, if you need to talk, if you are trying to be funny, ironic, sarcastic, sardonic or mocking.

We have more ways to communicate than ever. They are not good or bad. It's up to us to know how and when to use them.

If It's Not Nice, Don't Put It In Writing

True story. (Although I've changed people's names for reasons that will soon become obvious.)

I had a client who was really difficult to work for.

Let's call her Samantha.

I had a boss who had to deal with her regularly.

Let's call him Fred.

One day, Samantha and Fred had a meeting and Samantha was really hard on Fred. She was demanding and (truth be told) quite rude.

This meeting took place in front of me, which probably added to Fred feeling extra humiliated by Samantha's treatment. (Never admonish someone in front of others.)

Fred followed up on the meeting by venting all his feelings into an email for me.

He was a very good writer, so he told me in this email all the reasons why Samantha was (and I quote) *"an impossible bitch"*. The email was a caustic, sharp, particularly insightful thesis on Samantha and her ways.

Then, in thinking about her as he wrote this, he proceeded to send it to her instead of to me.

He came into my office about 10 minutes later asking what I thought of his analysis.

To which I responded, *"What analysis?"*

He went white.

He returned to his computer.

He yelled *"Oh, shiiiiiiit!"*

This is how Fred inadvertently taught me one of the lessons I am most grateful for: never, ever write anything in an email that you wouldn't be comfortable forwarding to everyone you know.

Never.

This way, if what you write gets sent to the wrong people or forwarded or copied and pasted or printed you have nothing to worry about.

How To Communicate Awkward Things

I remind myself that "awkward" is a feeling that I bring with me. I set the tone.

If I am acting tense, nervous, sheepish, I will make it worse. If I act confident and am direct, I will diminish it. A bit of grace polishes awkward right out of the equation.

Then, compassion. I try to put myself in the other person's shoes, not to guess or assume but to feel.

Next is intent. I don't want to hurt anyone or to intentionally make anyone uncomfortable. Coming from that space helps put things in their place.

Finally, I assemble what I want to say in the most simple, clearest terms possible. With tact, but without mincing words. No sugarcoating. No beating around the bush. If what I need to say is inherently painful the less I circle around it the better.

The Five People I Want In Every Meeting

The person who lays out very complex information or a convoluted story and *makes it look simple.*

This is the reverse of pretension and using flashy big words. It gets everyone on the same page, makes others feel clear-headed rather than inadequate, and it is beautiful.

When everyone in the room is looking at the same facts, the same data, and someone explains what these facts actually imply. I would call this skill an *information translator*.

When a person can see a pattern or a trend where others see unrelated information within the same field. An information translator that in addition ties everything together in a manner that is cohesive. I would call this person a *predictor*.

Maybe not always accurate, but always reasonable: the points are connecting in a way that is not forced or contrived; the progression is linear and laid out in a way that is compelling.

When someone sees information available to the rest of us in completely different fields and draws conclusions that to everyone else are not related to the information being shown, but then ties it back in a way that in retrospect seems absurdly obvious. The *visionary*.

When someone sits back and identifies what each person can do and makes sure their role in the company is consistent with their natural abilities. A *team builder.*

How To Talk To A Client

Your goal is to come across in a way the client feels you can be counted on.

From this place, everything becomes easier: the client regards what you have to say with respect and an open mind. It's more natural to be listened to. It's more plausible to push back.

As such:

Consider that your ability to manage a conversation with a client impacts everyone. When you speak to a client, often even in passing, you become responsible for sharing what the client wants with the rest of your team. This involves a clear understanding of what that is, what it will take to get there, and what the deadlines are.

Before this meeting takes place, prepare. Prepare yourself. Prepare the team. What will you say? How will you back it up? What do you dread? Who owns addressing what?

Is what you will talk about connected to the client's objectives? I'm sure you read this line and considered it a given. But this most obvious thing is a frequent point of failure.

Can you anticipate what might require further explanation?

You also own preparing the client. Does the client know what the meeting is for? Otherwise, how will the right people attend your meeting?

If you plan to surprise them in any way, don't. Instead, let them know beforehand about anything you think they might not be expecting.

At the end of the meeting, provide a summary, then follow it up with meeting notes. Make sure the notes are succinct and shared with the right people.

Consider meeting notes to be living documents. As things get updated, deadlines adjust and objectives shift, update the notes. They are intended to be a tool.

Make sure every communication with the client reflects organization and clarity of thought, as this reflects on you. On your emails include a clear subject line, a quick overview, and expectations. Don't assume anyone has time to scroll through an email thread.

Rather than thinking or saying "no", find the yes. This is not about saying yes to everything. It's about being resourceful. What are the alternatives? What are the options?

Never assume or conclude without direct communication. *"Here is what I'm hearing."*

Be present. Don't look at devices or get distracted when you are in the middle of a conversation. Half paying attention will never build trust. It also raises the risk of misunderstandings.

Before you update the team on your client meeting, make sure you truly understand what the client stated. Circle back. Ask questions. Don't rely on email. Listen. Make sure conversations have a written trail.

Don't ever hoard news, in particular bad news.

Be transparent. Be honest. Always, always, always play fair. This sets a precedent and builds trust.

It's never about being perfect. It's not about being infallible. It's about the integrity you handle yourself with when things go wrong.

How To Work Remotely

Over the years I have managed people who work remotely and do it so well I barely notice they are not in the office next door.

To write this answer I just had to get their input.

I requested from them and from my network the best tips they had to mitigate the fact of their absence.

Here are some of my favorites:

As with all things, the first step is the importance of establishing boundaries.

Working in an office provides breaks that we are not even aware of: the drive in, coffee down the street, a mid afternoon chat or a short walk around the block.

If you are working at home you sit at your desk long hours without moving or even looking up so establish healthy boundaries with your own schedule.

This way your contributions can be consistent and your time respected.

Don't burn out by working dawn to dusk with no breaks.

Before your job begins make sure you fly in to meet the team in person.

When you do so, spend time in one on one meetings and go out for coffee, lunch or drinks.

This is "in-person equity" that will help a lot when you are no longer there.

Arrange for a regular presence (once a month or once a quarter) and plan to be there for trade shows, conferences, milestones. Take advantage of times when travel is justified.

Make sure your employer is willing to invest in the right technology: video conferencing, Slack. These resources are essential to your success.

Communicate with your colleagues through multiple channels, such as Slack, Yammer, Facebook, WhatsApp, Zoom.

Your communication should be both formal and informal. Many important ideas and forms of collaboration happen over chats or banter.

Don't underestimate the importance of establishing social touch points that are unrelated to work.

Schedule coffee or lunch with a co-worker and eat and talk while on Skype or Zoom. This is not a meeting: it's time to be social and connect. It will really help you later when you will need to read cues, tone or establish the way something that was said in writing should be interpreted.

A friend sends a bottle of wine into the office mid-week with a card that invites her team to happy hour on Friday. They all toast (with her on the screen).

On this note, always be ready to hop on a video conference. If you receive an email and it seems terse or tense, call.

For these last minute decisions to take communication off email, a friend suggests always having a scarf and lipstick ready by the computer.

Establish a bracket of time where you plan to be "open to chatting" so anyone can call you to say hello and talk in a way that does not require a formal schedule.

At the end of the week send in brief, relevant activity reports to people on your team (not just your boss). It will help everyone visualize what you do.

What Does It Mean When A Person Says *"I'm busy"* Every Time You Want To Talk?

A few years ago I came across an article in the NYT titled *"The Busy Trap"*. In it, the author, Tim Kreider, noted that the most common response he received to *"How are you?"* was *"Busy."*

He said that this answer was delivered with a measure of pride but was disguised as a complaint, and that it was a way for the people who pronounced it to identify as important.

I am busy, therefore I matter.

Or, how can I possibly not matter, if I am in demand, completely booked?

How do we feel when we are not doing something? When we are not being productive? We feel anxious. We feel guilty. We feel like we are wasting time.

We overbook ourselves, over-promote what we do, and even overschedule our kids.

Remember when we used to play all afternoon?

Remember hammocks?

He observes the importance of being rather than doing, and how our brains work optimally if we are idle sometimes.

I don't know anything about you, nor do I know anything about this person who claims to be busy when you want to talk. No one has any context to answer your question (other than the person claiming to be busy).

The question, however, sparks another that we should all be asking ourselves.

Are we caught in "the busy trap"?

Is busy really all we want to be?

Reputation/Gossip

Reputation refers to how well you are regarded by the general population. It is related to your character, your estimation, your honor.

Reputation is cohesive, consistent, formed by an accumulation of experiences. It's collective, built by people who were there.

By contrast, gossip is petty, unreliable, conjecture. It's spread by people who speculate, who whisper, who claim someone else's friend of a friend witnessed what they describe.

When learning about someone else, consider their reputation. Ignore the gossip. Nothing will ruin your reputation faster than partaking in it.

What If Someone Is Being Confrontational?

I cannot change the fact that someone asks me questions in a confrontational way.

I can certainly help how I react to them.

I am one half of this pattern of confrontation — defensiveness. Without my repeated, predictable reaction, without the role I play, the pattern cannot survive.

If the confrontation has happened in the past, what is it about? What are the triggers? Do I see a trend? Can I then prepare for it?

Why do I react in such a strong way to this person? How can I be aware of my emotions so I can better manage them?

Once my emotions are less likely to instantly flare up I try to listen and to put myself in the other person's shoes. I really need to exercise empathy if there is any chance I can change this for good.

I believe that, more often than not, it's possible to arrive at a place where everyone feels understood.

How to Thrive as an Introvert

When you know yourself you are empowered.

When you accept yourself you are invincible.

— ***Tina Lifford***

A Few Of The Professional Advantages Of Being An Introvert

First, let's define the term so we're all on the same page: an introvert is a person who recharges by being alone.

It's not that we don't like social interaction or that we "don't like people"; it's that people deplete us. Even people we adore.

Here is a list of some professional advantages that we get just for being who we are:

Introverts are at their best when they're doing things that don't involve being in the midst of others. Luckily, many professions require solitude to get things done. A few examples: Writing. Research. Science. I'm sure you can think of many more.

Social media has become essential. Social networking tools are, in my opinion, tailor-made for introverts. We build extensive, meaningful connections via Facebook, Twitter, Quora, to name a few. We communicate, modulate our conversations, select what we want to engage in, all without ever being forced to interact with people in person. This might very well be my definition of heaven.

Introverts are thoughtful. We read and do research and ponder before ever venturing an opinion out loud, which means that when we speak up we tend to know what we are talking about. (This does not in any way imply extroverts aren't thoughtful. But it's true extroverts tend to think out loud.)

We are good listeners. It's not just that we'd rather listen than talk. It's that we operate in a world that accommodates extroverts so we have learned to pay attention to our surroundings in order to make it through the day. We notice things others don't.

Introverts have an aversion to small talk. This means that our conversations tend to have direction and purpose. They are oriented towards getting an assignment done, since talking for the sake of talking is not the best way to manage our limited ability to interact. (I bet you anything that Cinderella turning into a pumpkin was a metaphor for her just needing to go home and take off her shoe.)

Alas. Introversion is often regarded as a disadvantage, even a flaw, and nothing could be further from the truth. The world is our (quiet, peaceful, glorious) oyster!

Outgoing Introvert

I am social, outgoing and assertive and yet cannot recharge unless I find a quiet place I can retreat to.

In conversations with friends and strangers I mention right away that I'm an introvert because the "switch" from social and chatty to "I need to leave" happens pretty quickly and my life is better when those around me know that.

I write a lot about introversion and how the ability to identify what I need has improved my interactions and my relationships.

I write a lot too about telling the truth. I used to lie to skip social engagements without offending anyone and found that lying made it impossible for me to ever be understood.

Despite my efforts there are still many people who attempt to argue with me about who I am. (*"Dushka! You are mistaken! There is no way you are an introvert!"*)

The fact is this: no matter what I do or how I manage it, people will always talk. I will always be judged. (And so will you.)

All I can do is what you can do. Be who I am and communicate that as clearly as I can.

The reward is a clear, transparent life and a calm, quiet, empty space that is always waiting for me.

As An Introvert, How Can I Communicate Better?

Begin by abandoning the notion that you need to say something just to say something.

The most outspoken people are not necessarily the ones with the best ideas.

A person who takes her time to notice, to gather information, and then speaks up when she has something insightful to contribute is often the person with influence.

Rather than trying to do what someone else does, rather than falling prey to pressure that comes from a false sense of inadequacy, build upon the person you already are.

Who you are is not dictated by your ever changing, capricious surroundings. Who you are is dictated by you.

This matters for two reasons:

For your personal development, your setting should always contribute to making you a better version of yourself, rather than force you to be someone else.

If you fall prey to the against-the-current effort of trying to be something you are not, your own thoughts about how you are performing — how you are not enough — will constantly undermine you.

How can you ever make progress if your enemy is you?

Here is an example: you might feel like your contributions are always late. Notice instead that the most important developments always happen over several conversations, and that you have more time than you think.

Here are some ways I build upon who I already am:

I work hard at giving myself what I need because nobody else will (or can) do that for me. For me, this means going out of my way to make sure I am getting enough sleep. It means waking up early so I have a bit of quiet, peaceful time for myself. It means making sure I don't leave the house without breakfast.

If you think these things are not related to me bringing my best, most alert self into the office, think again.

I make sure I am prepared. I ask for a meeting agenda so I have time to think before the meeting starts. Once I am at the meeting, I look around and ask questions. I mentally gather information.

I'm always clear about who I am. People I work with know that I'm an introvert (as such they are less likely to interrupt me when I'm writing, expect that I will skip happy hour, get it when I say I need alone time.). I say things like *"I will follow up with contributions after I've had some time to think."*

Within running conversations, I carve out space for myself. When someone point blank asks me something and I know I have the answer but need some time to rummage around in my brain to organize it, I say *"Let me come back to that. I need to gather my thoughts."*

Finally, I dedicate time and resources to learning new things. You could take a training course about how to be a better presenter. Take an improv class to teach your brain to practice thinking on your feet. You can read books and articles that support the notion that who you already are is just fine, that you are already powerful in your own unique, wonderful way.

Convivial Sparkle

Last night I had to attend a networking event.

I stay away from 98% of networking events but this was not one I could avoid.

I asked my extremely extroverted friend Amit to please come with me.

Amit is all charm and social grace. He shows up in a cloud of convivial sparkle, walks right up to strangers as if he's known them forever, listens to them and then introduces them to each other.

As he walks away from one group to join another he makes sure he has left the previous group introduced, connected and with something to say to one another.

I find talking about myself somewhat gauche. I'm terrible with small talk so give short answers that don't really lend themselves to further conversation. I'm drained by what my brain interprets as senseless chatter so 10 minutes in I end up hiding behind the food table nibbling on crunchy toast.

Amit would have none of that. He ushered me around and introduced me to people in ways that would make it easy for me to talk to them.

Him: *"Dushka! This is Cindy and she just got back from Prague! You loved Prague!"*

Me: *"Hi yes I love Prague bye."*

Amit spent most of the evening talking about me while I stood there nodding and wordlessly handing people my business card.

Every introvert needs an extrovert.

How To Brainstorm Like An Introvert

I tell the organizer brainstorms are not what I am best at but that I will follow up a day later.

I ask if that deadline is acceptable. (It usually is because organizers need time to put all the chaos of ideas into something useful.)

I read the materials provided.

I do some research of my own.

I attend the brainstorm and take notes.

I process what I heard, then send my ideas/thoughts to the organizer a bit later.

I also want to note no one is noticing my lack of ideas. Most people are too busy worried about what people think of them to be concerned about me.

How To Network If You're An Introvert

Hello. My name is Dushka, and I'm a social introvert.

Here is what I can do:

Have coffee or lunch with someone one on one (where it's easy to focus and talk but also easy to quickly escape; rather than dinner/drinks that tend to linger).

Get to know them well.

Remain in touch with people I genuinely like.

Make introductions that matter.

Build extensive, meaningful networks via social media.

Text people.

Here is what I can't do:

Work a room (I feel queasy already).

Go to a "networking event".

Mingle.

Madly distribute and collect business cards.

Engage in small talk.

Attend or throw a party.

Pick up the phone when it rings.

How This Introvert Recovers From A Day Of Meetings

Managing my introversion is about more than recovery. It's about planning ahead.

Before the meeting:

If viable, I do not book meetings back to back but rather alternate with activities that don't involve other people (research, document development, contemplation of my inbox, getting my calendar organized).

I make sure the objective of the meeting is clear.

I develop an agenda.

I invite the right people to the meeting.

I keep attendees to an absolute minimum.

During the meeting:

I assign roles (Who is leading the meeting? Who is taking notes? The notes need to include action and owner and require follow up so the meeting serves a real purpose.).

I make sure the meeting is focused and as short as possible.

I encourage everyone to participate or provide input (there is a reason each person is in the room).

After the meeting:

If plausible, I take a short walk or even run a quick errand. (There is a secret bench near my office in a very quiet place, but I cannot compromise its location. I've already said too much.)

Rather than running from one meeting to another, I alternate meetings with getting things done that don't require others.

After the work day is done I rarely get together with friends, preferring to spend quiet evenings at home to recharge.

Often, when Boyfriend comes home, I'm sitting in a dark corner on a comfortable chair looking out into the San Francisco night.

Are Introverts More Open On Social Media?

I don't know if all introverts are more open on social media.

I know that's the case for me, because:

I get to engage on my own terms. (It's not like being at a party where you end up talking to someone you don't really want to talk to.)

I talk about what I know I can talk about. (I am abysmal at small talk so if I needed to engage anyone in small talk they would slowly but surely back away from me, horrified.)

I can interact with many, many more people than I could ever interact with in person, because the presence of another drains me. Social media exalts my social side while removing the parts of it that exhaust me.

I can make meaningful connections. I'm good at knowing who might benefit from meeting whom, so that rather than "working a room" (which I seldom find valuable) I can introduce people who can have a conversation that matters.

And my favorite:

I can leave any time I want. Leaving a party early (or not attending) can be rude, but on social media if I am feeling like I need to recharge I can.

Why does all this matter? Because social media is a networking tool and you don't have to ever go to a networking event if that is not what works for you.

Happy Hour:
An Introvert's Nightmare

A Friday happy hour with people I spend the entire week with sounds like my definition of hell.

I'd rather exercise, attend a cultural event, or travel. Instead, I feel pressure to suffer through small talk for political purposes.

I'd rather go home.

I'd rather go to the gym.

I'd rather read.

I'd rather do laundry.

I'd rather stay in the office and work.

For a while I would go anyway thinking it was important politically. What ended up happening is that it didn't help me politically because being somewhere I don't want to be does not show me at my best.

And also because if I keep doing things I don't want to do they add up and I end up in the wrong life.

Finally, I have found that the pressure I used to apply to myself was my own projection. At the end of the day it doesn't really matter if I go or not.

My co-workers have other concerns besides me, and see enough of me during the day for my absence in the evening to matter.

So I don't go. I openly say *"I'm an introvert and need to go home and recover from the week, but have fun!"* and then I'm free.

This has affected neither my career nor my relationships.

Your Resume and How to Interview

Choose a job you love and you will never

have to work a day in your life.

— *Confucius*

How Do You Distinguish Between A Good And A Bad Recruiter?

You can learn a lot about a person if you understand what drives her.

A good recruiter is a professional matchmaker who enjoys helping a company and the right candidate find each other across a crowded room.

A bad recruiter is motivated only by the commission they are getting today and does not bother with the long game: getting to know you or calling you back if the company has said they are not interested. This attitude betrays short sightedness; recruiting is a relationship business.

A good recruiter:

Can be trusted, is discreet, calls when she says she will, shows up to meetings and never fails to follow up.

Communicates clearly, asks the right questions, is direct, tells the truth and knows how to deliver difficult messages with grace. She is an ally, and the way she says things sheds light on what you need to work on for future interviews, such as *"The company did not think you were right for this position because when you said you were mostly interested in strategy they got the impression you would consider tactical work to be beneath you."*

Understands that her only client is the candidate, not the company who pays her. This is because if the candidate is assisted in finding the right job, everything else falls into place, including the paying company feeling like the money they spent was worth it because they found exactly the person they were looking for.

Wants to listen. She does a better job if she understands what you are looking for, the kind of job you want now and the kind of career you might want later, the jobs where you have been the happiest and the situations that tend to set you up to succeed. Good recruiters have been working with the same candidates for years, build networks, are well connected, and get recommended through word of mouth.

A bad recruiter:

Has no intention of talking to you. She reaches out without knowing you and without asking you anything; insists you look into jobs that you already know are not what you are looking for.

Does not have a good grasp on the job description and as such is unable to answer basic questions about what the company wants.

Takes advantage of your despair or lack of experience and insists the wrong job is actually right for you. This typically means that the candidates this recruiter recommends leave a few months after they are hired, which is bad for the candidate and for the company.

Is indiscreet, or gossips. You should be able to talk to a recruiter about the challenges your team faces, such as *"We believe a certain employee will be leaving soon and want to keep an eye out for how to replace him so that we are ready, but none of this can yet be made public."* If a recruiter reveals information that clearly should not be shared chances are high that she talks to others about things you have told her in confidence.

Doesn't follow through. If you don't get a job you deserve a call back, and a clear explanation as to why the company chose not to hire you. If this is done right, the recruiter can continue working with you on other opportunities and you will think to call her the next time you are looking for a job.

An Empty Resume

When your resume is empty — which is expected when you're just getting started — people interviewing you are not looking for aptitude or experience but attitude.

Are you curious? Helpful? Enthusiastic? Do you ask good questions?

Good hiring managers know that you can teach a lot of skills — and learn a lot of skills — but a good attitude is largely unteachable and very valuable. You have more to offer than you think.

Use a good attitude to start collecting what you are missing, which is experience.

Tips For Building A Resume

In general, what I most value in a resume is that I be able to quickly scan it.

Hiring managers look through several dozen resumes a day, so being able to at-a-glance discern if the candidate is promising makes the document stand out. (This can mean anything from putting the titles in bold to a candidate's tendency towards brevity.)

Whenever you can add quantities, do so. It paints a clearer picture of your abilities.

I suggest resumes tell a cohesive story where "overarching" accomplishments don't need to be teased out: most people have skills that pop out throughout their professional life that are only popping out because I am looking for them. Save me that effort.

For example, an ability to manage conflicting priorities, create order from chaos, simplicity from complexity. These should all be highlighted.

Along these same lines, disparate experience and volunteer work need to be made more relevant to the rest of your resume; not so much to falsely portray a single trajectory or unfaltering path but rather to reflect a singular person with distinct talents that are predictably going to show up in every job.

Every resume you send out should be tailored to the specific position, with your experience and qualifications. This brief narrative dedicated to the exact position goes where the objective once used to. That section should answer the questions: Why are you the right person for the job? What can you do for the company? (The answer to this is in your accomplishments.)

Think of your keywords (again within your accomplishments) so that recruitment management software picks up on your resume easily and for the right reasons.

Finally, consider a brief, tailored cover letter relevant to each position.

How Long To Wait For Your Interviewer

One day, many years ago, I had an interview scheduled to start at 9:00 a.m. At 9:45 I stood up to leave.

The person I was supposed to interview with caught me right as the elevator door was about to close.

I ended up working at that company for 14 years, and it was a wonderful adventure.

I'm glad I waited.

Things To Keep In Mind During A Job Interview

I used to treat interviews like a test. Someone sitting across from me asked me questions and I answered with the goal of demonstrating how much I knew.

This is an approach we learn in school. It forces us to assume a submissive role, one that wishes for approval; the person asking the questions is in a position of authority.

Now I approach interviews for what they are: a conversation between two people who are exploring if a professional relationship might be a good fit.

This means that:

The interviewer is trying to get to know me and I am trying to get an understanding of the organization. As such, I need to learn as much as I can about the company before I come in.

The questions go both ways. There are certain things I absolutely need to know before I can determine if I am interested in the job. For example, *"When can I meet the people who will be a part of my team?"*

If I don't know an answer saying *"I don't know"* ensures I don't end up in a job that is wrong for me.

Two other considerations:

An interview is wonderful practice. It gives me an opportunity to get better at presenting myself for who I am.

Interviews are really good networking opportunities, a chance to meet people in my industry.

The world is a small place and one day soon the person before me will be someone I get a chance to interview for a job somewhere else.

Is It Wrong To Lie In A Job Interview?

You are looking for a suit that fits and make an appointment with a tailor.

When you arrive you decide you want to impress the tailor with your imposing physique.

As he meticulously takes your measurements, you make yourself taller than you are, slimmer, stronger.

Do you know what ends up happening?

The tailor is not particularly impressed. It's not that you aren't imperial. It's that he doesn't care. He measures suits for many, many people. He's busy thinking about his own job and how he really hopes he can get home a bit earlier today.

You, on the other hand, walk the world with uncomfortable, awkward, ill-fitting clothes.

This is exactly what happens when you lie in an interview. You end up in the wrong job.

This wrong job is likely to lead you right into the wrong life.

Most people eventually realize that telling the truth is the way to happiness.

Representing yourself for who you really are is how what you are looking for finds you.

Interviews are a process for the person being interviewed, not the interviewer.

They are designed for you to find a job that's right for you.

What You Show

I had a friend who played football (soccer) every weekend.

Before making an important hire, he would invite the prospect to a game.

He claimed that he learned everything he needed to know about that person by watching how she played.

"But," I said, *"what if they are excellent at their job and just not good football players?"*

"It doesn't matter if they are good or bad. Are they courteous to others? Collaborative? During the game, are they lazy, or involved? Do they hide or are they eager to participate? Do they show effort, grit, enthusiasm? Do they show courage? Do they play a role in helping someone else score? Do they take all the credit and the glory? Who a person is somewhere is who that person is everywhere."

Does Quitting A Job Reflect Badly On Your Next Interview?

A job is not a life sentence. It is not a committed relationship. It's not you and me, together forever. It does not require vows.

Leaving a job is natural and does not constitute a transgression or even a lack of loyalty. Work is transactional: this is what I will do, in exchange for getting paid.

You can work somewhere and decide to leave in search of growth, variety, to learn different things, to exercise different muscles and even to meet different people.

You can leave your current job to step out of a rut, out of a routine, to stretch, test yourself, step out of your comfort zone.

Leaving is good.

How you leave your job is important. While in the job, do good work. Be engaged. Be accountable.

When you decide it's time to go, don't surprise anyone. Don't leave your team in a tough situation. Give plenty of notice.

If possible, offer to help hire and train your replacement. Ask the people you work with to be references for you.

What you say in subsequent job interviews is important. When I interview, I look for commitment (not life commitment, just a sense that you take responsibility seriously), I look for stability (not forever stability, but I don't want to again hire for this position in less than a year), I look for attitude and I look for competence.

The fact that you quit your previous job is something that I expect. Why you quit and how you did it matters to me a lot, because it might hint at how you will leave the position I hire you for.

"Trick Questions" In Job Interviews

When a company interviews you, the last thing on their mind is to "trick" you. They want to get to know you better and determine if you are the right fit.

Conversely, you are not there to answer questions. You are there to determine if the company is right for you.

An interview is an exploratory conversation, not a one sided interrogation.

Here are some of the most frequently asked questions during an interview and what I, the person conducting the interview, am really looking for:

Question: Why did you leave your previous job?

What I'm really looking for: I'm looking for you to reveal what it's like to work with you, because when we speak about others we are really talking about ourselves.

How to handle it: Say something honest that speaks to the future, such as *"I was ready for the next opportunity"*.

What not to say: Never complain or criticize the place where you used to work, or anyone you used to work for.

***Question:* What are you looking for in your next opportunity?**

What I'm really looking for: I want to confirm that what you want matches what I am offering. I want us to be compatible.

How to handle it: Make sure you study the company and the job description and go in with clarity regarding what they want to find. You too should be looking for the best possible fit.

What not to say: Anything that reveals a lack of connection between the company I am working for and the person I am interviewing. *"I just really need a job"* might be honest, but it doesn't help me determine why you are the best candidate for the job.

***Question:* Tell me about you.**

What I'm really looking for: I am looking for a quick summary of your work history, but I'm also looking to see what you highlight. Ideally, what you speak about with the most enthusiasm is what I need the most.

How to handle it: Make the answer as specific, focused and short as possible and ask a question back. *"I have been working in the communications industry for 20 years and am curious to know what the ideal candidate looks like for you, which would provide context for what I want to tell you more about."* Turn it into a conversation.

What not to say: Do not use catch phrases. *"I am a go-getter."* Do not launch into a detailed laundry list of all the things you have done. Long answers result in people tuning you out.

***Question:* What is your biggest weakness?**

What I'm really looking for: Everyone has weaknesses. I want to know if yours are compatible with my candidate search. For example, if the job is to lead a team thoughtfully, I don't want to hear you'd rather make a bad decision than no decision.

How to handle it: Do your homework, then be honest with a weakness that you really struggle with. *"I am enthusiastic and as such sometimes struggle to prioritize."*

Being honest with a weakness means you end up in a job that is right for you.

What not to say: Please don't say *"I'm a perfectionist."* Perfectionists are reluctant to try new things and as such don't grow as quickly as people who are less afraid to fail.

Question: Give me an example of a mistake you made and how you fixed it.

What I'm really looking for: Everyone makes mistakes. I want to know if you are self-aware and coachable. I want to see if you have courage and accountability or if you place blame on others.

How to handle it: State a mistake, own up to it, then explain how you found a solution. The whole answer should be both clear and brief.

What not to say: "I never make mistakes. And I never would have made this one if it hadn't been for my boss, who consistently used me to cover his own ass."

Question: What salary are you looking for?

What I'm really looking for: I really want to know how much you want to see if under my budget limitations I can afford you.

How to handle it: Choose a range that's fair and that would make you happy for the next 365 days.

What not to say: Candidates who answer this question clearly are always taken more seriously than those who refuse to answer.

Question: Where do you see yourself in 5 years?

What I'm really looking for: I want to know if you are a long-term player. Attrition hurts my business.

How to handle it (if you don't have a 5 year plan): "I am looking for a position where I can ideally grow within the company. In 5 years I hope to be learning and growing."

What not to say: "I don't know." It's OK not to know, but it doesn't help distinguish you from other candidates.

Question: Why should you get this job?

What I'm really looking for: A top line summary of your strengths and how clearly you deliver them.

How to handle it: Rehearse. Have this answer ready. The general message should be "the attributes you are looking for match my natural strengths, and my track record proves this."

What not to say: Something that reflects you're thinking about yourself and not the company. *"Because I am the best"* is less impressive than *"because I know how to contribute to the company exceeding business objectives".*

Bonus tip:

Once a company determines they want to hire you they will ask for references. Don't just give them the contact information: follow through. Call your references and say *"This company is specifically looking for someone to lead their team. I would really appreciate it if you could highlight the work we did when I lead xx project, and how I handled making sure everyone felt listened to".*

My Favorite Interview Question

I'm going to skip the part where I tell you good interviewing skills are critical because hiring is — you know. The right person changes the game and the wrong person is like a train wreck that destroys everything in its wake — regardless of level — and what you'd really like is for your interview to predict which the person sitting across from you is going to turn out to be.

Plus, you've hired the wrong person before.

And you will again.

While predicting the future is a noble undertaking, and while the company you work for should have in place a methodology proven to come close, what can you do as an individual to make sure that your insight contributes to a more fortunate hiring process?

(A lot, actually. But I'm going to stick to the subject, so will focus on this one little sliver.)

My vote for best interview question in the world is:

Give me an example of a mistake you made and how you fixed it.

Most common answers:

I can't really think of one right now.

I haven't made mistakes in a while.

(Gasp) *I did make a mistake, but it wasn't my fault.*

(Double gasp) *I did make a mistake, but it was her fault.*

(Triple gasp) *I made a mistake but it was because I was following orders.*

I can talk a lot about the second part of the best interview question in the world ("how you fixed it"). This alone reveals quite a bit about the candidate's troubleshooting skills, her creativity, imagination, resourcefulness, thought processes and her ability to work within a team.

But my favorite is the first part: "give me an example of a mistake you made", which is, without exception, followed by an audible intake of breath and a pregnant pause.

Within the answer to this first part of the question, I'd like to see a sense of humanity. An acknowledgment of fallibility; a sign that the person has already met with and recognizes her limitations as a mere mortal. If you never made mistakes you would not be flexible, nor adroit at mending broken things, nor well versed at assessing risk. Even worse, an individual who cannot own a mistake can't learn from it, which is a good indicator of the person's ability to grow within an organization.

I'd like to see accountability, with maybe even a tiny, healthy tinge of possessiveness. *That mistake was mine, all mine, and I have no one to blame but me.* First, because it's safe to say that a team member who points fingers before they even get the job does not bode well for a collaborative team environment, but more importantly because if you assign blame to someone other than you, you relinquish your power, and I much prefer working with powerful people.

I'd like to see courage. *I am so scared you will think less of me if I tell you the stupid, stupid thing I did and maybe decide not to hire me but I'm going to tell you anyway because you asked and my mistakes are part of who I am so if you decide because of them not to consider me for this job maybe you're not the right company for me so here it goes.*

I'd like to see a sense of humor. A woman I interviewed once replied *"Just one example? Today alone I made about four mistakes before I'd even had coffee!"* and proceeded to show me that her socks didn't match. (Although now that I think about it, the look was sort of bohemian chic so maybe she was showing off.)

I learned this very handy interview question because one sunny morning, a long, long time ago, someone asked me to provide an example of a mistake I had made and how I had fixed it.

My answer was, naturally, that I tended to not make any.

That was what I said, in part because I was really young, but mostly because I wanted very much for everyone to believe that I was perfect. (I have since aborted the mission because I was perpetually exhausted and because I found out later that no one was buying it anyway.)

Which brings me to something else you need to remember about people when you interview them.

I hear over and over again the adage "people don't change". But you know what? Everything changes. The weather even after you check your really accurate new app, your intentions even if early this very morning you were brimming with resolve, your feelings despite being so vocal about the certainty deep in your heart, your preferences because when was it that Brussels sprouts became so delicious? Your plans because, as you have already noticed, nothing ever turns out how you anticipated; even the precise interpretation of the promises you made, because that was then and this is now.

So it's only logical to conclude that people do indeed change.

Go ahead and ask me to give you an example of a mistake I made.

Just make sure you set aside some time.

How An Introvert Can Do Better In A Job Interview

Things I do before the interview:

A day or two before my interviews I spend plenty of time alone so that I feel lucid and well rested rather than already depleted.

I find a way to promote myself that doesn't involve (ugh) me telling you about my good work. How can my work speak for me?

For example, I provide a long list of references and make sure I talk to them so they know what part of our experience working together should be highlighted.

To be specific: *Do you remember that week when we had several different deadlines that we had to meet on the same day? This job demands someone who can handle conflicting priorities, so it would be great if you can tell them about that.*

I think about what I can bring to my interviews that can represent me. Lately I bring copies of my books. They give me something to talk about, which is easier than small talk, and I can leave behind writing samples.

I prepare with the specific objective of making the day easy on myself. If I can get the names of the people I will be talking to I can look them up and take some notes of specific things to talk about with each of them.

I ask not to meet too many people on the same day. If I have to interview with more than four people I request doing that over the course of two days instead of one.

The more I know the easier the day of the interview becomes so whenever possible I go on what I will call a reconnaissance mission. This way I know how to get there, how long it will take me, and maybe even what the building looks like.

Things I do on the day of the interview:

I make sure I'm early. This reduces stress and frazzle and gives me time to sit somewhere quietly.

I mention the fact that I recharge by being alone.

I ask a lot of questions, which for me works better than small talk. More importantly, we are interviewing each other. Just like they want to know if I am right for the job, I in equal measure want to know if this job is right for me.

What I do after the interview:

I send a note to the recruiter thanking her for the experience.

I send each person I spoke to a thoughtful, personal note and connect with each one on LinkedIn.

Interviewing is a great way to network. Even if I am not right for the job, even if the job is not right for me, other great things can come from the fact that we met.

My Interview With A Stay-At-Home Mom

A stay-at-home mom recently blew me away with her interview.

Here is what she did:

She very specifically listed all the things she did in her current job (as a mother) and explained how they directly applied to what we were looking for. (For example: *I can handle conflicting priorities. I can multitask. I am good at a wide range of things. I get everything done.*)

She explained how the time off had given her a vantage point/point of view that made her an asset. (For example: *By being a woman and a mom, I became the target audience for these companies who should be trying out "x" to better promote themselves.*)

She anticipated concerns people who were interviewing her might have. (For example: explaining how committed she was to her responsibilities, and how she had remained in touch with work related matters, the news and colleagues all along.)

She was very candid about her boundaries. (For example: *I cannot travel, but once I put my kids to bed I'm happy to work late to get the presentation done if that is what is needed.*)

Finally, she was not apologetic about her choices.

We hired her.

How To Accept Rejection

I once interviewed a candidate I really, really liked.

Unfortunately his skills and experience were not the right fit for the specific job I was interviewing him for.

We had to turn him down.

He called me requesting feedback. He felt the interview had gone really well and liked the company and the people he had met.

He did not understand why we had not made an offer.

Our reasons for not doing so had nothing to do with him. They were due to our very specific needs, internal dynamics, and other circumstances unrelated to his ability, personality or performance.

I am telling you this because in every rejection (a job, a girlfriend, a friend) there is at least some disrelation between you and the reason for the rejection.

Understanding this separation between you and being rejected is how you learn to accept rejection with grace.

Your First Job

The usefulness of the cup

is that it is empty.

— Bruce Lee

My Very First Job

My priority for the very first job I ever had was this: *where can I learn the most?*

As an intern, I saw many things.

People vying for projects with the most visibility.

People fighting over the bigger office.

People trying to figure out how to get a better salary or a promotion faster or working out how to make the best impression with the least amount of effort.

Forget about all that.

Being where you can learn the most will serve you well forever.

What Tips Could You Give To A New Employee In Their First Job?

I find starting a new job to be absolutely terrifying. I want to instantly and all at once deliver on all the promises I made during the interview process, which hypercharges every move I make. Everything is new. The simplest things are so complicated.

What is the name of the person who just remembered mine? How do I find the documents I need? Where did you say my desk was?

Here are some things I do to make the first day easier on myself:

Take the edge off. I take the edge off my first day by learning as much as I can before I start. I read. I inform myself. Whenever possible, I set up coffee dates with the people soon to become my co-workers (on the days preceding my first day), so that when I start I don't feel surrounded by strangers.

I arrive early. On my first day I'm always early. I walk around the block, I take a breath, I do everything I can to avoid the distress and frazzle of being late. I'm already nervous enough.

I find a buddy. If the company doesn't do this for me, I identify a buddy, a friendly face who is not my boss who can help me with basic things. *Can you remind me of the code to get through the door? Can you tell me again where the bathroom is? How can I reserve a conference room?*

I get the lay of the land. I ask someone for a tour of the office or I walk around myself to make it easier for me to find obvious things. Where is the printer? The supply room? Where does my boss sit?

I get to know my team. I spend a lot of time observing my team members. I know my strengths and weaknesses well and realize that we are all better together. Who can I complement? Who complements me? Finding where I fit in the team puzzle will make everything better.

Mind open. Ears open. My thoughts don't let me hear what is happening around me. My expectations close off possibility. I try to set these things aside to make room for the very real adventure I am beginning.

I avoid gossip. I can't stress this enough. If I begin to hear people talk about others — not in a helpful, informative, contextual way but in a petty, diminishing way — I step away.

I introduce myself. As I walk around getting familiar with my surroundings I introduce myself to people, stating my name and my new role. I defy all the times I have said *"Oh, I'm terrible with names"*. Get good at it, Dushka. It's not OK to not know the names of the people around you.

I ask a torrent of questions. Everyone around me knows I am new and has a certain level of tolerance for obvious questions. I take advantage of this window to ask whatever I need to know.

I learn. I am here to learn. This applies to my job, but also to my life. It is so much better to approach things with an open mind than it is to pretend or assume to know. I am an amateur, and I want to learn more than I want to impress you with my knowledge.

Set aside the imperative of making a good first impression. If I am focused on trying to impress people I make it all about me. Instead, I listen. I will sound a lot smarter if I begin to talk *after* I have absorbed what is happening around me, a few weeks from now, than if I start giving opinions from a place of ignorance. I lack context, and will lack context for some time.

I set boundaries. If I say yes to everything, answer emails in the middle of the night and work weekends, that is what I will teach people to expect from me. What are my boundaries? The time to define them is now.

I stay a bit late. I don't stay late in the office to impress others. I stay late if I have a reason to. But in the first week on a new job I like to spend some time taking notes of my day, organizing what I am going to do the next day, and making sure I have a clear sense of priorities. I like making tomorrow easier and, who knows? Maybe someone new will start tomorrow, and I can offer to be their buddy.

I Just Landed My First Job But Feel It's A Step Back Since I Want To Be An Entrepreneur. What Should I Do?

A full time job and being an entrepreneur are not at odds with each other. They are not a dichotomy. One is not a distraction from the other.

Full time jobs have taught me pretty much everything I know. What is working here? What is not? How did this company that hired me go from small to big? In that trajectory, what has it lost? What is it doing well? What are the things I should never, ever replicate? What inspires people? What kills their spirit? What affects creativity? What is it that the world needs the most?

There are many ways to get from here to where you want to be. Every way is full of answers and offers the tools you need to assist in the expedition that is your life.

You will miss receiving the most essential, most necessary things if you embark on this believing that you are betraying what you really want.

Instead, open your eyes. Learn as much as you can. Do good work. And believe this: the path is everywhere.

My Boss

My boss has a view of work that is more holistic than mine. We both have our areas of expertise, but mine is vertical and specific, and his is more horizontal, comprehensive.

I am learning how to think in a way that is more cross-functional and connected, and attempting to process it as if it was a metaphor for my life (because everything is).

He has a tremendous work ethic and is thorough and detail-oriented and yet unfailingly makes room to consider another person's insight or opinion.

The ability to be neck deep in something and both willing and able to extract himself and be receptive to what others have to say is what I am going to call a notable example of workplace compassion.

I admire other things about him too: his self-awareness and ambition. He's very direct and I never wonder what he is thinking or attempting to tell me. We talk without having to hide.

While I personally consider this a basic requirement (hiding things and being different things to different people fragments me and as such I don't do it), I also think it's a privilege to not ever have to worry about cloaking anything that I am.

He expects from me what I can potentially do, rather than expecting that I replicate things I have done. I consider it a confirmation of my good fortune that the person I report to believes in me. If he thinks I can get there, then I happen to agree. Consider for a moment what a gift this is.

My boss is a big reason why I accepted a full time position at the wonderful company I work in. We become like the people we surround ourselves with, and my hope is that who he is rubs off on me.

Is The Boss Always Right?

Imagine that you have someone who reports to you. She is both younger and less experienced than you but is remarkable at research and at other things you don't usually make the time for.

When you tell her what to do, she, in a non-confrontational way, outlines what she thinks would be better, more on point, more efficient or targeted. Her point of view is enlightening. You realize time and time again that she is right.

Personally, I would love such a person on my team. I would ask for her opinion and would be more than happy to correct my course of action if I felt her insight was better.

I have asked this question to people time and time again — *what would you do with someone like this on your team?* And nine times out of ten the answer is *YES PLEASE I WOULD LOVE THAT WHERE CAN I FIND SOMEONE LIKE THAT.*

Senior people at companies are so very busy. They want solutions; answers, not questions. Less work, not more, and to make less decisions. They want things to be taken care of. They want one less thing to worry about.

This can only mean one thing: everyone around you is open to you telling them what to do if what you say is smart, well informed and replete with common sense.

A boss who pushes back on this and prefers to "always be right" will get stuck. He will be left behind so fast he will eat everyone else's dust.

A person who solely because of his position claims to always be right would not be someone I would work for.

What One Thing Makes Someone A Very Mature Person?

Imagine if you will that two employees are relatively new to a company and are experiencing the same thing: people around them are disorganized, distracted, and massively busy.

They each go to their supervisor.

One meeting goes like this:

"I feel like nobody likes me. In fact, everyone hates me! No one will even look at me! Nobody wants to help me. Honestly, I think coming here was a mistake. Why is the world so unfair? Why can't I ever get a break?"

The other meeting goes like this:

"Wow, this place is so exciting. Everyone is so busy. Can you point me to online resources — such as an onbourding document — so I can figure things out without having to take up anyone's time? Also, can you help me sort out how I can be most useful? It sure looks like people could use the help. It's just that sometimes you are too busy to even delegate, and I think that's where you could orient me the most."

If I were to pick a single sign of maturity it would be the ability to move past myself so that I stop taking things personally.

Is Being Coachable Important?

There are so many things about you that nobody knows but you.

But.

There are so many things about you that everyone knows but you.

How do you come across? How do others perceive you? How do you get in your own way? How can you round out the person that you are? How can you improve, grow?

People provide feedback all the time.

You have to be willing to listen and be receptive to making a distinction between what is worth listening to and what isn't.

This receptivity — this self-awareness combined with an ability to listen, filter and apply what you hear — is what makes you coachable, and it's essential to your success.

It's very difficult to address your shortcomings if you are unaware of what they are.

I have been an executive coach and media trainer for 20 years.

For a living I tell people how they come across and how they can communicate more clearly.

I have seen over and over that the most successful CEOs are open and listen and nod and take notes. Even within an aura of knowledge and power they are humble and avid to learn more about themselves.

The less successful CEOs assure their teams they do not need coaching. They claim they know everything already and shut out feedback from people who have something they lack: an outsider's perspective.

My job has taught me that being coachable is essential to success.

Rumors

Whenever I hear someone has been saying something about me I get this urge to FIND. OUT. MORE.

I want to know everything, every single bit, and get a chance to be heard so I can clarify any inaccurate information.

That's when I remind myself: what others say about me doesn't matter.

I need to keep my focus on myself, my own priorities, interests and trajectory.

What people say about others reveals more about them than about those they talk about.

A Glorious Misunderstanding

When I was little I was uncomfortable with the fact I had to ask for things.

For permission, but also for money for every little need or whim.

For me, money was less related to *buying* and more related to *doing*.

It was an enabler.

The first time I got paid it was for an article I had written about the experience of being a Mexican teenager living in Beijing.

Don't tell anyone, but I write all the time so I would have written it anyway.

The fact that I was getting paid for something I did for pleasure seemed like a colossal, glorious misunderstanding.

I held that paycheck, looked at it incredulously and laughed.

Then I felt free.

Since that day I have never again asked anyone for anything. I can get it myself.

How You Know You Are Good At Your Job

Internal indicators:

No Sunday blues.

You don't dread Mondays.

You wake up in the morning with a sense of purpose in relation to your day ahead.

You feel connected. There is a clear, clean line between you, your day, your work and what matters to you. It's not "work you" and "weekend you". It's you.

It's not "work-life balance." This is the continuous line of your life.

There is a sense of flow to your day. Things fall into place with ease but you feel challenged and on your toes. Things aren't "easy". It's more about a place that you inhabit between difficulty and ease.

You are always learning something new.

You feel proud. *"Damn. This document is good."*

Your work has a natural, organic sense of evolution.

Forget about other people. These are the things that really matter. It's between you and you.

As a bonus, external indicators might be:

Positive feedback not just from your manager but from people around you.

A sense of harmony. Even when you work hard, really hard, there is no sense of swimming against an invisible riptide.

And, the truest, most democratic indicator that you are doing well: You have a lot of work.

People who are good at their jobs attract more work.

You have a lot to do, and many things are not even in your job description. Can we have your thoughts? Your insight? Your opinion? We need you. Because, you know what? This could really use your touch.

How You Know You Are Bad At Your Job

Internal indicators:

You feel dread. You dread going to work.

You are at work and wonder *oh my god what the hell am I doing here.*

You ask yourself if this is all there is and dream about running free across green fields.

You go out of your way to cut corners.

You find fault with everyone and everything. You complain a lot about what a bad job other people are doing, how ineffective they are, how your job would be better if they were doing theirs.

You get home exhausted, listless, even if your job is something you can get done almost out of habit.

You are mostly on automatic, and this applies to other areas of your life.

You feel stuck.

External indicators:

A bad performance review. But, beyond that, you feel excluded and out of the loop. You don't belong here. Your work is always the same — over and over — but the amount of work seems to be declining.

You clock in and out.

How To Use Your Morning Effectively

Most of the people I know who stick to exercising regularly do so early in the morning. They do it before their day gets in the way, and then they are done.

It sounds perfect, except it doesn't work for me. I wake up groggy and my body feels stiff and it takes me 30 minutes just to warm up.

If I exercise in the early evening my workout is much stronger. At the end of it I am relaxed and clear headed. It helps me dust off my day.

I crave the chance to move and stretch after being at my desk so it feels like a reward rather than something I have to force myself to do.

I used to love writing at night. My house was dark and quiet and I typically wrote until late. Now if I write at night it takes much more effort. I labor over a text I would get done in under 20 minutes if I did it right when I get up.

If I write first thing in the morning writing comes so easily.

If I need to schedule meetings or time with friends, it takes a lot out of me early in the morning where I am more productive if I can be by myself. In the evenings I'm too tired from the day to be social.

I tend to schedule meetings in the middle of the day.

If I schedule an early morning coffee with someone, or do automatic tasks (like cleaning my house), I feel like I am wasting my brain when it's at its most lucid.

The most important thing I have learned about time management is that different things work for different people and that if I get to understand my very individual, ever changing internal cadence I can take advantage of it in a way that is uniquely my own.

How Do You Stay Healthy When You're Busy?

I realized that being healthy was the sum total of small choices. By this I mean it's less about grand gestures (I will run a marathon!) and more about the day in, day out decisions. For example, I make it a point to take the stairs.

I make health a priority. It's too easy for me to decide I don't have time, I have more important things to do, there is always tomorrow. But I can make time, nothing is more important than this and all I have is today. I put "yoga class" on my calendar, just like I would a meeting.

I plan ahead. Cooking on Sunday so I have healthy food to reach for during the week is the only way I don't end up eating whatever. (Chips. I mean chips.)

It's not about willpower. I don't have the stamina to expect sheer willpower to be what pulls me through to a healthy life. I admit it: I like pleasure, and I recruit it as a motivator. What healthy food do I find delicious? What exercise do I look forward to? What else motivates me? I am more likely to stick to things I enjoy.

It's easier not to buy than not to eat. If I am hungry or in a rush I will reach for that bag of chips on my kitchen counter. It's easier not to eat it if I don't have it in my house.

I give food its sacred place. Food is pleasure, comfort, solace, communion. I recognize this, so I pay attention to it. I make space for it. I try to eat, just eat, rather than eat while I'm doing other things. Extra points if I eat with a friend (rather than with my email).

There are things I don't do. I don't stay up late. I seldom drink. I don't do drugs.

I get a general check up once a year. This also goes on my calendar.

I define health broadly. It's not just about eating a lot of plants. Am I stressed? Why? How can I change my approach or my perspective? Am I getting enough sleep? (Don't ask.) Am I constantly pushing myself? (Yes.) Am I gaining weight? Am I spending too many hours at a desk without moving?

I watch my social interactions. Do I have relationships that make me happy, that fill me rather than drain me? Do I surround myself with people who love me, support me, accept me? Am I paying attention to my friends? Am I too worried about what others think of me? Am I too concerned about approval?

I spend time with myself. My life is demanding. A large percentage of it is output. If I am expending energy, what is it that recharges me? For me, that's time alone. If I give myself that, I sleep better. I work better. I think better. Spending time with myself puts everything in its place.

The Impact Your First Job Has On Your Career

When it comes to your choice of profession or your career path your first job doesn't matter.

People switch careers all the time and it offers the hiring company a diversity in approach and point of view.

If it relates to your character, your first job matters forever. So regardless of what you are doing or how transient you consider your first job to be, remain accountable, deliver on your promises, be reliable, follow through, work hard, be a good team player and treat others well and with respect.

Avoid gossip and speaking ill of others.

These are the building blocks of your reputation, and that is about to become your most valuable asset.

Media and Presentation Training

Wise men speak because they have something to say.

Fools speak because they have to say something.

— *Plato*

How To Be A Better Presenter

People tend to respond to questions like "how can I be a better presenter?" with a laundry list of advice (and it's usually quite good).

But here is the truth: the right advice depends on the person.

Here is a fairly radical, counter-intuitive example: some people do very, very well if they rehearse a lot. For them, "practice" is invaluable advice.

I have been training high level executives (CEOs and C-suite) for long enough to confirm that this is the case for most people.

There are also people who are at their best when they wing it. Rehearsing (or over-rehearsing) makes them more nervous. It makes them come across as stilted or artificial.

If through training someone I discover this, my advice is *"please stop rehearsing"*. It works like a charm.

Their presentation is unlikely to be highly polished; but it tends to be engaging and human. They become good presenters in their own, unique way. Not slick, not flawless, not neat. Still good.

Here is the most common misconception: we look at a good presenter and decide we need to look/sound/come across like that.

Most of us have the potential to be fairly decent presenters, but not like someone else.

We can be good presenters in a unique style that is all our own.

Good presentation training stays away from general advice and refuses to try to make you sound like someone else.

Good presentation training brings out who you already are.

I guarantee this: being who you are out there in front of everyone is way less scary than feeling you have to go out there and act like somebody else.

Improve Your Presentation Skills, Improve Your Life

If you remember nothing else, remember this: if there is no emotional connection between the presenter and the material being presented, there will be no connection between the presenter and the audience.

During a presentation training session a lot of the work I do is related to content, to the rearranging of the slides themselves in an effort to re-establish or strengthen this connection.

Often, the slides are developed by one person (or team) and presented by another. This has a tendency to create a chasm between the content and the presenter.

A presentation intimately belongs to who presents it.

Know what you want to say. This is one thing, maybe two. The rest of the presentation wraps around this central point.

If you want to say a lot more than that consider a white paper, a contributed article series or a book.

Understand who you are speaking to. What you want to say might not change a lot, but how you say it has to appeal to your audience.

To capture their attention you are in a very real competition with their mobile devices.

Be who you are in real life. The very common advice to "be more animated", or "be more enthusiastic" or "be more polished" will not work if it's not who you are.

You can be a good presenter in your own individual style. A good presentation trainer will help you find it. You should not be trying to sound like anyone else.

No effort you ever embark on should involve trying to be someone you are not.

I mean this in life, not just during your presentation.

Do you know the single most important ingredient in connecting with your audience? Chemistry. PowerPoint arrests the attention from you to a bunch of slides, effectively neutralizing your most powerful tool. If you must use slides, use them sparingly so the eyes are on you.

Figure out what makes you comfortable. I get questions like this all the time: *Should I walk around? Use a podium? Should I use a teleprompter? Is eye contact important? Should I look at the camera? What should I wear? Is it OK if I say "ummm" a lot?* My answer is: there are always best practices, but if what I suggest makes you uncomfortable it does not work for you.

"Do what makes you comfortable" trumps any other advice.

My favorite part about presentation training is that it is a metaphor for life. If you want to be a good presenter, re-establish your interest in what you do, be who you are, think of others instead of what interests you.

Take really sound, really wise advice and rather than asking yourself *"is this good advice?"* ask yourself *"does this work for me?"*

If it doesn't, I don't care how good it is. Throw it out.

The Truth About PowerPoint

I don't know about you but when I know I'm about to see someone else's PowerPoint presentation, my first thought is *"Oh, no"*.

By slide four, what I'm usually thinking is *"I don't care"*.

Then, I check out.

Too often PowerPoint presentations are mind-numbingly boring.

It's not supposed to be this way.

As presenters, in exchange for the gift that is our audience's attention, the least we can do is inspire.

The most important element required to accomplish this is connection.

As a presenter you are not only fighting for your audience's full attention. You are competing with their mobile devices.

You have to be compelling enough that no one tunes you out or looks down at their phones while you are speaking.

For connection to have a chance to make contact, your audience has to be looking at you and you have to be looking at your audience.

A PowerPoint deck tells people *"Don't look at me. Look at my slides."*

PowerPoint blocks connection.

It extinguishes chemistry.

The way to write a successful PowerPoint deck is to remember what it's for.

It's there to support, to highlight, to make it easy for the audience to follow what you are saying.

It's not there for you. It's not there to remind you what to say or so that you can read the slides.

PowerPoint is not for the speaker. It's not your framework, your structure or your talking points.

PowerPoint is for the audience.

In particular, it's for the audience to barely notice it's there.

My Product Has Enormous Advantages Over What Has Gone Before. How Do I Boil This Down To A Single Soundbite?

Here is what you need to be ready to say about your product.

In very simple terms, what problem does it solve?

In equally simple terms, why is it different from your competitors?

In equally simple terms, what are the benefits?

In equally simple terms, who says your product has many enormous advantages aside from you? Analysts? Customers? A third party — someone other than you — has to enthusiastically agree with what you say about your own product and be willing to talk about it.

Don't explain all the complexity of your product and leave the punchline for the end. Start with the punchline and then elaborate from there.

Speaking about your product is not a gimmick. It's not about a soundbite. It's about focus, about simplicity and about relevance.

You Know You Do That. But Do You Know Why?

I am giving a presentation training to a very tall man.

When he is sitting before me he has a multilayered, open, fascinating personality but when he moves to the front of the room he seems to dwindle.

If he stepped into his entire presence he would be mesmerizing and I realize I need to better understand the why behind what he is doing before explaining what I see.

Telling him how he comes across without a reason might not help him and could undermine his confidence; this is the opposite of what I want to do.

"You are very tall," I say. *"Do you find you make yourself smaller so that others don't find you threatening?"*

"Yes," he says, surprised. *"I've done that all my life."*

"I understand the reason behind this but it's interfering with your ability to present. I realize I am asking that you undo years of hard learned social behavior but can you not do this while you present?"

With that feedback he goes to the front of the room again and the difference is pure splendor.

Presentation training (or any type of executive coaching) that focuses on small things like your body language or where to stand but that doesn't get to the source of your behavior and how it undermines you cannot yield lasting results.

Understanding why you do what you do will impact your presentations forever and might even change your life.

Nervous Before A Presentation?

When I was little, feelings ruled over me with an iron fist.

I cried when I was hungry. I hollered when something felt scratchy. I ranted when my little brother played with my toy.

It was later that I decided that the best way to deal with feelings was not to feel them. I didn't want this crush, this heartbreak, this loneliness, this isolation, this anxiety, this sense of not fitting in anywhere.

Tell me how not to feel inadequate.

After many attempts at developing a metal-cold, harsh, uncaring, aloof personality, what I came to discover is that the more you push feelings away the more they persist.

Feelings are implacable.

Feelings are not intruders. They are an inside job. This is why they are such experts at convincing you they call the shots.

I can't. I can't resist texting the guy who just dumped me.

But, you can.

I can't. I can't give this presentation because I am absolutely terrified and I just can't.

But, you can.

I love all my feelings and welcome them and make room for them, even when it's hard, even when they are vile.

But I am the boss.

This is the secret to asking someone out on a date while your knees are shaking. This is how you do things when you are not motivated and would rather stay in bed. This is how you deal with (allegedly) paralyzing fear. This is how you get up on stage when you feel shy.

The recipe for you to not feel what you are feeling does not exist.

You feel shy. You do it anyway.

How Presenting Makes Me Feel

Before the presentation:

Someone asks me to do a presentation. The subject is something I feel strongly about and I express interest in the opportunity.

Details are sorted out and the gig is confirmed.

A few days before the presentation:

I feel stressed about this. It would have been easier to decline.

The day before:

Ack. Ack! WHY DID I AGREE TO DO THIS? WHY DO I KEEP DOING THIS TO MYSELF?

A few minutes before the presentation:

OH MY GOD I CAN'T BREATHE I CAN'T THINK I HAVE FORGOTTEN WHAT I WANTED TO SAY WHAT IS MY NAME?

Right before I walk on stage:

WHERE IS THE BACK DOOR I WILL ESCAPE I WILL RUN FREE NO ONE WILL EVER FIND ME I WILL POST ON QUORA FROM REMOTE LOCATIONS!

As I see people clapping after someone introduces me as the speaker:

OK. OK. I can do this.

Two minutes in:

Huh. This is fun! This is actually fun.

In the middle of the presentation:

OH WOW I LOVE THIS I LOVE EVERYONE I AM SO HAPPY THIS IS MY LIFE BEST DAY EVER!

Towards the end of my presentation:

I WANT TO TAKE EVERYONE HOME THEY ARE ALL SO BEAUTIFUL!

As I walk off the stage:

I am so hungry.

After food is provided:

I need to go home and sit in a dark corner forever. Please go away.

Another opportunity that is right for me will come and I will take it. It's a good chance to show my fear who is boss.

What Is Media Training For?

Have you ever watched an interview and felt that the person being interviewed was not really answering the question?

Have you ever heard a podcast, lost interest and switched to something else?

Have you ever read an interview in an article and remained unsure of what the person being interviewed was talking about?

All these people needed media training.

Media training is what people do when they want to learn how to talk to media.

It usually involves general tips and good practices, but mostly "dry runs", where a person who used to be a reporter (or can act like one) allows the spokesperson to practice in a realistic setting.

The goal of a media training is to communicate more clearly, to explain what your company does (in a compelling way) and how your company's products are different from the competition.

A media training can be done in many different formats depending on needs — most frequently it is tailored to specific requirements — and can be imparted to many different people across the same company.

The most common are:

A crisis training. The company is going through a crisis and spokespeople need to quickly learn how to communicate clearly, honestly, effectively and consistently.

A one on one session with the trainer and the CEO of a company to prepare for a specific interview with a high-level business publication, such as *The New York Times* or *The Wall Street Journal*.

A training that includes the whole C-Suite. This is a very useful team building exercise, where what needs to be said or highlighted about the company is tested, explored, evolved and agreed upon.

A training for a few people in the product team to prepare them to talk to tech press, sometimes in advance of a launch of a new product or to prepare for a trade show (such as CES).

Other uses for media training: often, people hire a media trainer to prepare for an important job interview; or use it as an internal training for a stellar employee who could use tips on how to communicate better with co-workers or teams.

A good media training can be life-altering. Here is why: we can all learn how to communicate better, and when we are told by a professional how we come across and how to be more clear it tends to have a positive impact across more than one area of our life.

What Are The Biggest Mistakes Executives Make When Talking To The Press?

You begin answering questions based on the assumption that people are interested in what you have to say. People are not interested in you. People are not particularly interested in your company. People don't necessarily find interesting what you find interesting. People are interested in how your thoughts and experiences apply to them. This is relevance.

You don't have a "why". A conversation with media has to have a reason. I don't mean a "sell". I mean an objective, a point of interest, a problem, an observation. What is the angle here? What is the story? What do you want to say, and why do you think it matters? This is impact.

You live on an island. What is happening in the world outside your company? What are the industry trends? How does the story that you are telling fit into this larger, much larger, picture? This is context.

You expect media to take your word for it. Media is skeptical. They are trained to take what you say with a grain of salt. They will do their homework. They will talk to industry analysts. They will talk to your customers. They will talk to your competitors. Whenever possible, validate your story through third parties.

You confuse talking to the press with selling. Talking to media is about your story. It's about the problems your company and your products are out to solve. It's about the industry and non-obvious ways you see it evolving. I know you want to sell your product but if that is your intent you will get transferred to the advertising department, or worse. You will spend time and resources on an article that no one will read.

You forget to speak in plain English. Don't use acronyms or words that mean nothing. Don't use marketing speak, legal speak or corporate speak. For example, do not claim to have a *"proprietary leading utilization landscape with data sets that provide end to end benefits."* Use English. Just English. Have a conversation.

You neglect to direct the interview. I am not suggesting you ignore the question. (This is frequent and terribly rude advice. Don't do that.) I don't mean you should strong-arm the reporter into talking only about what you want to talk about. What I mean is you know your story better than anyone and as such it stands to reason that the journalist might not know exactly what to ask you. *"Before we begin with the questions, do you mind if I give you a quick overview of why I think our story is of interest to your audience?"*

You play games. You practice "bridging". You "deftly" skirt the question. You pretend you answered, and then skipped it. You made something up when in fact you didn't know. Please don't play games. If you don't want to answer, say *"I would rather not answer that, and this is why"*. If you want to focus on something else, say *"I would like to focus on something else"*. If you don't know, say *"I don't know, and I will get back to you"*. Don't insult someone else's intelligence. It won't end well.

You don't prepare. Make a list of your nightmare questions, all the ones you really hope never come up. (They will come up.) Prepare answers for them that are brief and honest, or failing that, determine how you will handle them (for example, by declining to comment and explaining why). This is a lot better than looking stunned at a question you could absolutely predict.

Wishful thinking is not effective.

You speak off the record. Nothing is off the record. Even if the interview is over. Even if the cameras are off. Even if you have left the room and are chatting in the elevator. If you are going to say something, assume it will make it into the article.

You lie. People will find out. Trust is like Humpty Dumpty. (According to Lewis Carroll, *"All the king's horses and all the king's men could not put him back together again."*)

You refuse to talk to press. If your story is interesting, it will be told. Do you want to play a role in how it's told?

What Is Your First Lesson About Talking To Media: A Summary

Summary: The basic rules of talking to press are the same as the basic rules of talking to anyone.

Here is what I mean:

Keep it simple. What do you want to say? Why do you want to say it? What do you want the outcome to be? Say what you want to say. Don't bury it in garbage words.

Tell the truth. Nothing will keep people from understanding you more than them not trusting you. Loss of trust is almost impossible to recover from.

Listen. Look at the person talking to you. Don't think about what you plan to say next. Don't plot your counter-argument. Don't glance at your phone.

Be polite. If you are pushy, forceful, tactless, snarky, rude, you will create a noisy interference that will impede you from getting across what you want to say.

Be brief.

Don't assume. If you are deducing, suspecting, estimating, expecting, stop. Don't guess. Ask. Confirm.

Focus. Don't multitask. Don't think of what you need to do when the interview is over. Take a deep breath. One thing at a time.

Don't play games. Don't bridge. Don't repeat things over and over. Don't avoid the question. Don't distract. Don't do one thing to accomplish another. Don't strategize to manipulate the outcome. Stick to saying what you mean.

Be interesting. The only way to accomplish this is to stop thinking about what you find interesting and start thinking about how you can make it interesting for another. It's never, not ever, about you.

What Are Your Best Tips To Prepare For A Live Television Interview?

Know your audience. Who watches the show? What are they most interested in? Collect the information you need to understand how to frame your story.

Remember that it's never about you, even when it's all about you. Focus less on your company, less on you, and more about how what you are here to say applies to others.

Understand the format of the show. How long will your interview be? What questions are you most likely to get? Have they done any research on you or should you begin with a short introduction? Can you send your interviewer questions you'd like them to ask you? (Typically, you can.)

Be clear on what you want to say. Forget about "messages". Be succinct. Tell a story. Be visual. Use anecdotes. Draw a direct, obvious line between what you are saying and why it matters.

Headline what you want to say, then say it. *"Once upon a time, there was a little girl called Little Red Riding Hood. She wore a red coat with a hood and was fond of strolling across the forest..."* will have less impact than *"Little girl, attacked by wolf. Wolf dressed in grandmother's clothing."*

Practice. Develop soundbites through "headlining" what you want to say (like the Little Red Riding Hood example above). A sound bite is brief, catchy; and typically "packages" a lot of what you want to say. Have someone film you a few days before your interview so you can look at yourself and become more aware of your body language and facial expressions.

Prepare answers to your worst questions. What questions keep you up at night? Writing out how you would handle them is more helpful (and effective) than pretending they will not come up.

Be here now. Tell yourself that for the duration of the interview you will not allow your own brain to distract you. Set aside your worries, your problems, what you will say, what they will ask you next. Focus on right now.

Wear comfortable, presentable clothes. Put yourself in a place where you will not think about what you are wearing. If your clothes are too tight, too uncomfortable, if you have to constantly tug or adjust, that is what you (and your audience) will zone in on. Don't wear white — the camera adjusts to light colors and the rest of you will look washed out. Don't wear patterns; they are distracting.

Bring your personality. Ignore anyone who tells you to sound "more excited", "more alive", "more like X celebrity". You cannot come across as credible or authentic if you attempt to sound like someone other than yourself.

Don't look at the camera. Looking at the camera is terrifying and disorienting. Also, it's hard to tell which camera is on so you could be staring deeply in the wrong direction. Instead, look at the person talking to you and shut out everything else.

Just before you go on, take a few deep breaths. Breathing deeply tells your body that despite the nerves you are not in danger.

Am I Doing This Right?

A person who has never made a mistake has never tried anything new.

— Albert Einstein

Is This Uncomfortable Or Is It Wrong?

Getting out of your comfort zone feels terrifying in a thrilling sort of way. You don't want to do it but you really do. The voice in your head says *"I can walk away but if I do I will wonder about this forever."*

Wrong feels like NO. Like anger. Like resentment. Like this is not at all who I am. I am compromising myself, I am doing this for the wrong reasons, and if I do this I will regret it, but more importantly, I will like myself less. I will be ashamed. This doesn't feel like an opportunity. This feels like a mistake.

Things I Wish Someone Had Told Me

Attitude is more important than experience.

Networking events = waste of time.

Networking events are not a good way to network. Discover your own personal way to meet people relevant to you and stay in touch with them, preferably because you genuinely like them.

"Working a room" is rarely going to be worth the time.

It's about what is happening out there in the world. Not what we do in here in our offices.

Curiosity is where it's at. Go explore. Travel. Devour books. Develop a point of view.

We live trapped in an echo-chamber of our own creation. Get away from the reverberation and go get something fresh.

On this note, put your devices down. Look up.

Work is a roller coaster.

You will be hailed as a hero one day, and as an incompetent disaster the next. Develop your own sense of what you are worth early and don't heed neither criticism nor praise.

Let me know when you've successfully figured out how to do this.

Things will bounce back at you so fast you'll get whiplash.

Your intern will be your boss (someday very, very soon). And I hate to tell you this, but your boss will be someone you come to understand better as the years go by, regardless of what you think now.

Don't regard peers as competitors; don't concoct rivalries. We are all in this together. I believe this to the bottom of my heart and it's one of the principles that regulate how I do business.

Examine the reason — the real reason — behind the decisions that you are making and behind what's affecting you at work. Your ego will get you every time. Make your ego an advisor, not your master.

Then show me how.

Trust the people you work with.

Assume they will do a good job and they will rise to the occasion. Check everything they do and tell yourself that you and only you can do it right and they will second guess themselves constantly.

Say yes.

One of the most interesting things about life is that you don't really know what you like, and what you like is quite possibly going to change. Say yes to that assignment you think you are not interested in. At worst you will learn something you wouldn't have been exposed to otherwise.

Let life surprise you.

What Makes A Good Mentor?

A mentor is someone who has already walked down the path you think you might be interested in and as such can help guide and maybe even inspire you.

The relationship usually takes the shape of regular meetings or calls where you might talk about things you think about, that concern you, that interest you, that trap you or that stop you.

Your mentor listens, asks the right questions (also known as "active listening"), and without directly giving you advice shares what worked for her so that you might decide what to apply to your life or situation.

The intent is for you to learn how to listen to yourself rather than become reliant on what another person has to say.

"I, like you, also wondered if this was what I wanted to do with my life. I knew that I did because I woke up looking forward to going to work", rather than *"You should absolutely do this. I loved it and I know you will too."*

Another very valuable thing your mentor might do is make an effort to introduce you to the right people to network with, to work for or even to talk to.

The dynamic between your mentor and you should be relaxed, comfortable and pleasant. A mentor is doing for you what she wishes someone had done for her so meeting with you is full of meaning, like a large circle being traced and closed. It should never feel like tension, like an imposition, or like a favor you have to in some way pay back.

Nothing about the relationship should feel pushed, forced, or coerced. If you feel aggression or an attempt to get you to do things you have not had a chance to think through, or if you feel your actions lead to somehow benefit your mentor, these are signs that you are being manipulated.

Your mentor should help you stand on your own two feet and believe in yourself rather than admonish you, criticize you or diminish you. No one should do these things but least of all someone in a role meant to support you.

You should also watch out for a term first coined by Sigmund Freud known as transference. It's very common and what happens when you feel a strong attraction towards someone in a position of power.

Any person with authority — a mentor, a teacher, an instructor — should know that getting romantically involved with a student or a patient is a serious breach of ethics, because it takes advantage of someone in a vulnerable position.

Your relationship with your mentor should feel good. It should be something you look forward to. It should ultimately inspire you to pay it forward and be a mentor to someone aspiring to walk in your footsteps.

What Does An Executive Coach Do?

Too often we are busy with what's urgent and lose track of what is important in the day-in/day-out grind of our responsibilities.

Then we look back at our week and realize we've been putting out imaginary fires and accomplished nothing.

Or, we do a job well and get promoted into a position where every task seems unfamiliar. (Have you noticed how promotions sometimes take people from a job they are excelling at to a job they have no idea how to do?)

Working with an executive coach provides the space we need to step back. It lends perspective to our work, allows us to identify where we are putting our efforts and see if these at all relate to where we want to get.

Sometimes we need another person to tell us that if we keep doing what we are good at instead of doing what we are afraid of we will never grow.

A third party who has no skin in the game can tell us exactly how we come across (did you know that being intimidating is not synonymous with leadership?), assist us in navigating change, or help bridge the areas we are finding difficult.

Executive coaching sessions can be focused on developing the skills required of a new position — such as management skills — that might not have been a requirement in a previous position.

The time with an executive coach can be used to identify what employees do to get in their own way, hindering their growth.

We all get in our own way.

Executive coaches work with people who feel stuck or who lack confidence or who are scared or who don't listen or who worry so much they can't make decisions or who make decisions too quickly.

Or, work with employees to improve upon areas that have been identified with their managers, such as working better with others, or working better alone, or working better with a team that is remote.

The sessions can be tailored to help get an employee to the next level, which often requires the development of a new perspective.

You can't get to a new place by doing old things.

Executive coaches sometimes work with employees to find a new place for them within (or even outside) an organization, when they want to do something different but have not been able to identify what that is.

No one can tell you what that is, but a good coach can help you find the answer within yourself, or be at peace not finding it, or have the courage to do what you know you need to do.

In a general sense, an executive coach helps an individual go from where they are to where they want to be, ideally in the service of their organization.

Things Managers Do That Drive People Crazy

It's my experience that people are not afraid of hard work. We all take pride in being challenged and are motivated by learning new things.

It's pointless work people cannot stand.

If work is unnecessary, or more elaborate or complex than it needs to be, that breeds resentment.

We already know the importance of recognizing good work and giving people promotions and raises.

Promoting someone before they are ready or offering a raise more related to circumstances than merit (in an effort to keep someone from leaving, for example) has a tendency to backfire.

We all appreciate recognition when we know we deserve it, but it seldom works as a manipulation tactic.

Employees welcome being guided or supported. Everyone despises being micromanaged.

At its core, micromanagement is interpreted as *"my way is the only way to do this right, and no one can do this better than me"*.

As stellar as you might be, this is seldom the case.

The best thing you can do is trust that you made the right hire and get out of the person's way. Trust, but be there to support if necessary.

Note that this implies that a lot of your value as a manager begins with an effective recruitment process. You can't just delegate recruitment to another department. It needs a manager's full involvement.

Observing an employee and recognizing where they are strong — seeing them for who they are so you can put them in a place that plays to their strengths and develops their potential — is a particular kind of talent and is generally deeply appreciated.

Just don't pigeonhole people. They are always more than what you see.

Recognize that there has to be an evolution to your one to one management style. The same person who deeply appreciated detailed direction one day will really need you to get out of her way a few weeks later.

Or, conversely, the person that you take for granted will do flawless work will need you if you ask them to do something new to them.

Be a leader. Have strong opinions and make decisions. Decisions by consensus, more often than not, first slow down an organization, then kill it.

Do keep open ears, though. If you listen to people, regardless of level, they will improve upon every decision that you make.

Stay away from anything that is in any way fake, such as making an effort to be liked or requesting someone's opinion on a course you already decided on to feign consensus.

Insulting someone's intelligence is never effective.

Look at the person beyond what they do for your organization. Recognize that they have a life beyond work and remember people matter more than companies.

When making decisions — or helping an employee make a decision — look at the whole person.

When my very best people come into my office with a job offer that is better than what I can provide, I tell them (with a hand clutched over my heart) that it's time for them to go.

They might not stay on my team, but they stay in my life.

Things Employees Do That Bother Managers

Trust is the glue that holds a team together.

Be reliable.

Follow through on your commitments.

Do what you say you are going to do.

Tell the truth.

Err on the side of clarity.

Meet your deadlines.

People are counting on you.

Complaining releases enough energy to dispel the worst of your frustration and ensure you have only enough motivation to continue complaining but do nothing about what you are complaining about.

It seems small, maybe even harmless.

Wake up. It's a trap.

Complaining is a form of paralysis and the worst form of procrastination.

Resolve to fix what's bothering you instead.

Be respectful.

This encompasses everything from reading the agenda in preparation for your meeting, to showing up on time, to being prepared, to avoiding interruptions.

Say what you need to say.

"I feel overlooked" is better than gossiping, rolling your eyes or looking angry.

Write well.

Bad grammar reflects poorly on both you and your organization.

Resolve to get good at taking feedback.

This means listening to what others have to say and then saying *"thank you"*.

Being defensive or taking things personally makes things difficult for everyone, most of all you.

Blaming others is the quickest way to lose your power, not just in the office but in life.

Point the finger back at yourself.

Be efficient.

This means making things easier for others.

Avoid long, unclear emails, meetings with no objectives, eternal conference calls where everyone resorts to doing other things.

Follow up.

If someone asks you to do something, it's not done until you report back to the person who made the request.

Assume that if it needs to be improved, it's your job to improve it.

Why Can't I Understand Things Unless They Are Explained In Detail?

I have two very different team members.

One emphatically nods the moment I start to talk and is ready to jump on the task before I have finished explaining it. I've noticed she processes things by doing. Throughout the execution of the assignment she asks more questions and checks in often.

The other needs a lot more time. She exhaustively interrogates me. She asks things that are often so obvious she can come across as intractable or difficult — it's almost like she is disguising an argument with question marks.

But let me tell you. After a long conversation she goes off and produces work that is stunning in its insight and thoughtfulness. I have learned to spend any time with her that she needs. The end result is better than anything I could ever do.

Be patient with yourself. We all take things in differently. Respect the way your brain works. Give yourself what you need.

Understanding all the layers is what puts you in the best position to get the job done right.

Networking Is Not What You Think.

"Networking" is not something you have to go to a "networking event" for.

It's not related to being exposed to new people or handing out business cards or knowing how to "work a room".

Networking is what happens between you and the people you work with. It's day in, day out. It's what you show to the intern in your group, how you treat the people who work for you, how you relate to your peers, what senior executives perceive.

Time goes by and everyone goes to work somewhere else, most frequently in your same industry or an industry that overlaps with yours. They grow. That intern becomes your key client, the people who used to work for you become someone you now work for. Those you considered senior report to you.

It's a small, small world, and your network — the web of "people you know", the social infrastructure that will matter the next time you need something (a tip, advice, an introduction, a hand, a recommendation, a reference, a new job) — is assembling itself right now.

How To Solve A Problem

Solving a problem requires that I do two things that are completely counterintuitive.

One, that *I identify what it is I believe in that is not true.*

But, if I believe in something, it's very, very difficult to recognize that I might be wrong about that belief.

Two, that to find a solution to a problem *I might need to look at this problem differently.*

This is hard because the only way I know how to look at something is the way I already do.

In both cases I have to step outside myself in order to see.

I seldom meet someone eager to prove herself wrong, and this is what makes it so hard.

I remind myself as often as I can that my perspective is real.

It's just that it's not all there is.

I am just one point of view in the midst of a universe of multiple perspectives.

I find so much solace in this.

Whenever I find myself facing a problem with "no solution", I try to step out of my perspective. I talk to others.

I ask myself, *What is it that you are not noticing? How can you look at this differently? What are your basic premises, and is it possible that any one of them is not true?*

It stands to reason that solutions are to be found in all the things I do not know.

How Do You Coach People Who Know More Than You?

Imagine a very smart person standing on top of a hill. She can see everything: the hills, the valleys, the houses, the sky.

She can see everything. She can see much more than me. But I can see her.

Under The Lamppost

A drunk loses the keys to his house and is looking for them under a lamppost. A policeman comes over and asks what he's doing.

"I'm looking for my keys" he says. *"I lost them over there."*

The policeman looks puzzled. *"Then why are you looking for them all the way over here?"*

"Because the light here is so much better."

We all look for things where the light is better, rather than where we're more likely to find them.

I try not to set specific goals. To be receptive to the opportunities life presents to me.

To open my eyes. Say yes more often.

I try not to wear blinders on my only adventure.

How Not To Be Everywhere All The Time

For years I believed stress made me more awake. My system was on perpetual high alert. *"You are the person I'd most want with me in a crisis"* was music to my ears.

I was convinced anxiety increased my efficiency and productivity. What a colossal mental trap. It's impossible to let something bad for you go if you are secretly convinced it's precisely what makes you valuable.

I could never sleep well, or even rest much. I was exhausted all the time, perceived danger where there was none, and came close to burning out.

What saved me was discovering the power of being just me instead of attempting to be everyone's superhero. Of being here now instead of everywhere all the time. And breathing. My breath, available to me at any time. Bigger. Deeper. Slower.

There was no decrease in productivity as a result of these revelations. What I feel instead is focus.

I am not indispensable, I am not invaluable, I am not all things to all people and I don't save the day.

I am doing more, much more, except it's coming from a place of purpose instead of that dark gaping lie of a hole where nothing can ever be enough.

To Commute Or Not To Commute

For ten years I commuted from a town near Half Moon Bay on the California Coast into Mountain View; then, a few years later into San Francisco.

It took about 80 minutes each way, and I was used to it so considered it no big deal.

Then I moved into an apartment in San Francisco. Instead of driving into work I took a bus, where I could spend 20 minutes catching up on email. This extinguished my commute to nothing.

The first week of living in this apartment, I was shocked at how much I managed to do and how early I got home. How was it only 8:30 p.m.?

It took a full week for me to realize that this was my life minus the three hour round trip every day. It was like adding another day to my week.

I resolved never to commute again if I could avoid it. A house sounds wonderful but time is life and as such it's no contest.

Try To Look Professional

Someone once told me I would have to keep my hair short as my naturally misbehaved, curly hair was not "professional".

To me this is less about my hair and more about the message that who I already am is somehow inadequate.

Throughout the years the length of my hair has varied.

There has never been any correlation between how I do at work and how long my hair happened to be at the time.

My Mantra

Just do a tiny little bit.

Take a big goal and break it into really small steps.

Don't feel like going to the gym?

Run 10 minutes. Maybe five.

Want to start writing a book but don't know how?

Write a page a day. Or a paragraph. Or a sentence.

Big goals are overwhelming, which leads to a state of total paralysis.

Small steps get the job done.

Every Day

I'm so tired. Wrung out. I've been writing and writing and writing and it feels like I have nothing left to say.

I want to go outside. I want to play and walk in the sun and stretch out my back and release my shoulders and gently bend my fingers back, one by one.

I want a neck massage.

Instead I sit my ass down on my chair and write.

Today, what I write is crap. It's not getting shown or published or submitted anywhere.

But I will write it anyway.

I have been writing long enough to know I will have bad days and good ones and I have to push through the bad ones and rejoice the days that all I want is to bound to my computer, the days it almost feels like I'm taking dictation, that someone is writing through me.

Ah, the days of flow, fireworks and glory.

I'm an amateur writer and it's never motivation that gets me through.

It's discipline.

Every day no matter what I sit down and write.

Then, when a beautiful, guileless soul tells me that they are envious, that they wish they could write like me, so easy and so effortless, I smile and say thank you.

Why Is It Tough To Get Work-Life Balance?

I was drowning in work.

I was convinced this was because my job was demanding but as I shuffled my responsibilities around, switched jobs and ultimately became a freelancer so I could call my own shots I was still drowning, drowning in work.

It finally caught up to me that it's me. I have a tendency to drown myself in work and the problem is not the job I'm in.

One of the reasons why work-life balance is hard is because we attribute the problem to our environment when it's us. I am the problem.

I adore making my clients happy. *"Dushka, your work was incredible." "Dushka, we would not have survived without you."* This is primal. Me, a kid, making someone I love proud. *Good girl.*

What can get in the way of work-life balance is that approval often matters more than the balance I claim I want.

I am ambitious and want to do great things and as soon as a project is done I'm hungry for the next one. I want hard work. I want to push myself, test myself. I want to learn.

Sometimes work-life balance is hard because there is a discrepancy between what I say I want and what I really, truly want. I'm sending everyone mixed signals, including myself.

I don't know what I want. I want conflicting things. I want everything.

My life is constantly changing. If a friend is visiting from out of town I want to work less, if I happen to be particularly inspired I want to work more, if a family member needs me I don't want to have to worry about work at all.

Work-life balance is hard because my definition of it is a moving target. It means different things to me depending on where my life is at.

What is work-life balance, anyway? Does it mean I get to go home every day when the clock strikes 5:00? Does it mean that I work hard for a few weeks and then take a long weekend off? Do I want daily balance, or do I want things to balance out over the course of a few weeks, even months?

Sometimes work-life balance is hard because my demands on it are a poor fit in relation to the job that I am in.

Work-life balance can be hard if you believe that the only way to do something well is to do it yourself. This means you can never delegate, and as such you are not scalable. Your ego gets in the way of you being free, and it gets in the way of the growth of everyone who works for you.

Work-life balance can be hard if you are worried someone else can do your job better than you. Then you live in a constant state of suspicion and paranoia and never allow yourself to step away. Your fear is calling the shots, not your lifestyle ambitions.

Work-life balance can be hard if you are more worried about looking good than doing good work. If you want to make sure everyone sees you are the last one to leave, if you want to make sure everyone is a witness to you being the first person in the next morning, what others think of you has more weight than your aspirations of getting home in time for dinner.

My boss assures me that employees come first, that people are the most important thing, yet I don't see him telling me it's time to go home after lunch because I worked really late the night before.

Wait a minute. Why should my work-life balance be the company's problem, in particular if I've already identified that my needs are ever-changing? How can I expect someone else to stay on top of that? The only person responsible for me is me.

Work-life balance can be hard because blame is easier and much more comfortable than accountability.

The Worst Advice

A friend once told me no one could outwork him.

"There are smarter people out there than me," he said. *"People that are better prepared. People that are better connected. But no one can work harder."*

Admit it. It makes sense.

It took me years to realize his formula for success, while tempting, is a fallacy.

It sounds so intuitive. Work harder. Stay later. Work longer. Work more.

We even have an acronym for this feeling that haunts us when we suspect we're not doing enough: Fear of Missing Out. (FOMO)

But a frenetic pace doesn't lead to success. It leads to burnout.

Any effort to do more to avoid "missing out" leads to an increased fear of missing out.

We will always be missing something and trying to not miss anything will make this fear unquenchable.

We require down time.

No wonder we feel hopeless and disenchanted. No wonder we are so scattered, distracted. No wonder our brains go on automatic.

No wonder we go to jobs we're not engaged with.

We're tired.

The secret to increased creativity and inspiration is not more work.

It's rest.

Get Some Rest

Aside from my beloved morning cup, I stay away from coffee. If I am feeling like I need it through the day to wake me up, what my body is really saying is that I need more sleep.

I go out of my way to make sure I am getting enough sleep. I go to bed early, I have no screens (such as TV) in my bedroom, and on weekends I reserve time for naps.

If what I am aiming for is productivity — or even the creativity required to be more productive — I look at my day and remove all the meetings that are not essential, where my role is either not clear or not necessary. I cannot do work if I am always in a meeting.

At my desk I switch from one task to another. I intersperse meetings with calls with document development so I can remain interested and focused and fresh.

Alternately, and depending on the task, I block three hours of solid time so I can focus all my attention on a single thing. This is particularly true when I am writing.

I take breaks. Small breaks to stretch and walk around, long breaks to go out for a walk or out to lunch. Breaks clear my head.

After work I engage my brain in other ways that are not work related so whatever parts of my brain are busy at work can get some rest.

I make sure I get enough exercise. We were meant to move, not sit at a desk scrunched over a computer.

I unplug and remove myself from work over the weekend, resist the temptation of using Sunday afternoons to "catch up."

I make a point to take vacations so I can focus on a completely different world from the one work offers me.

Let me tell you what all my points have in common: rest.

The biggest lesson I have learned about productivity is that constantly pushing myself to do more does not lead to more. That's not how humans work.

Never underestimate the power of a well rested you.

Does Going On Vacation Mean You Don't Like Your Job?

Does plugging in your devices mean that they don't enjoy working for you when you use them?

Does that sound preposterous?

You are like a device. Enjoyment is unrelated to the fact that you depend on your ability to restore your energy levels.

Recharging is essential to your functionality, to your power and to your performance.

Except, you are much more complex.

Recharging — taking a breath, taking a break, taking a vacation — doesn't only empower you to return to work, it lends you a sense of perspective you can't get if you don't step away. It revitalizes you, inspires you, reinvigorates you.

Taking a vacation means you respect yourself and respect your work and are committed to bringing forth the best of you.

Your Career, Or Love?

A woman who was reporting to me came into my office to ask for help.

"Dushka," she says. *"There is an opening for someone with my qualifications in our office in China. Can you please help support my transfer?"*

Me: *"I'd support anything you were really interested in. Would your husband go with you?"*

Her: *"No. He's working for a start-up and feels it's important to stay."*

Me: *"But, you've been married less than two months. Please give this some thought. It's a really tough thing to do to a relationship. Listen: good jobs come and go. Finding a husband is a once in a lifetime thing (ideally)."*

Her: *"We've talked about it, and we really want to do this."*

So, against my better judgement, I help her transfer. Inwardly, I know they are making a really big mistake.

Time goes by. I see their posts on Facebook. They are having a candle-lit dinner together via Skype. They are on opposite ends of the world, and every few months meet in a new "midway" location so they are traveling a lot. They look so happy. She tells me they are in touch multiple times a day.

Then she calls to tell me her year is up, that she's ready to return. She says she learned so much, and got to visit many places she had always dreamed of. The fact that her experience is now more international is a huge asset to my team.

I find out through reading the news that his very successful start-up sold for millions and millions of dollars.

How is that for giving someone the wrong advice?

Sometimes you feel you have a choice to make between two opposite things and the truth is that is rarely the case. Choose to have it all, and then make intelligent decisions to make it viable.

Morning Person

All my life I was a night owl. I worked best very late, in the dark and in the quiet.

The night distorts things somehow and I felt this somewhat altered perception worked to my advantage.

Through the years things began to shift. I was tired all the time, unable to pay attention or remain alert.

I discovered with wonder how much better and more lucid things looked in the morning, how easily documents allowed me to edit them with none of the bleary-eyed strain of the night before.

It didn't happen quickly but it happened absolutely.

I became a morning person.

When I first switched from a full time job to a freelance arrangement the thing I craved the most was having my precious mornings to myself. I woke up early to write and to sit at my dining room table peacefully, doing nothing.

I found supreme inspiration just knowing I didn't need to rush anywhere.

After a few months I realized that once I got up and sat in front of my computer it was hard to pry myself away from it. It took increasing amounts of effort to get out of the house to interact with other humans, to make it to a yoga class and in general to not become to a complete, wild-haired hermit.

The arrangement that had worked so well gradually began to isolate me.

"Dushka," Boyfriend observed. *"Your already tenuous level of tolerance for social interaction is plummeting. This can't be good for you."*

I decided to switch things around. To get up and go to yoga first thing, come home to shower and write, then leave the house in the early afternoon for work sessions.

For me the answer to being at my best is to listen to myself. Whatever system works after some time begins to fail me and needs to be rethought or switched around.

This is in part because routine allows my brain to go on automatic.

Turning off my brain kills my focus and my drive.

Creativity is a fragile thing and thrives whenever I change the environment it has gotten used to.

Ways To Stretch

Remind yourself that just because something doesn't make sense is no reason to not do it.

Find that book that you thought might be too difficult for you to read and crack it open and tackle page one.

Go against what someone who loves you wants for you but that you don't want for yourself. Disappoint the person you least want to disappoint in the name of honoring who you are. It will break your heart.

Let what you want determine your actions, not what you think others will like.

Talk to many people who believe you can do more than what you think you can do and open your ears.

Find the stretch job, the one you think you are not quite ready for, and go interview.

Raise your hand. Speak up. Stop speaking only inside your head, nodding to yourself because you know you knew the answer but no one else could hear.

Ask him out. Tell him how you feel. Tell yourself how you feel.

Leave that person who continues to hurt you. Stay with that person who continues to teach you. If they are the same person don't ask anyone — not anyone — what to do. Figure it out.

In fact, stop asking others anything you should be answering for yourself. You decide.

When you make all the decisions, you will make a ton of mistakes, even if you follow your gut. Everything will often become a spectacular catastrophe. Welcome to your life.

Is anything health related haunting you? Make a doctor's appointment. Get it checked. Run the tests. Rule it out. Right now, not soon. Not tomorrow.

Stop leaving for later what you don't want to do. But most of all, stop leaving for later what you've always, always wanted to do. Otherwise it won't get done. Not ever.

Mind Shift

One of the biggest mind shifts I've ever had to do was fully own the fact that I am the one who decides.

I see this at work a lot: what keeps a junior employee from becoming a manager is the ability to shift from asking a lot of questions to answering them. From *"What should I do?"* to *"Here is what you need to do."*

This agency is the main ingredient in becoming an adult. It's not that you suddenly know more — we are all winging it — it's that you come into the fact you have both power and free will.

We like asking for permission because it releases us from responsibility. *"Tell me what to do"* is less scary than deciding.

What should I do with my life? What should I study in college? Should I break up with him? Should I be angry? Do I stay or go?

Often we ask for advice because we are hesitant to be fully responsible for the consequences.

The price to pay is that you are giving your life away to others. Your life is in effect the sum of the decisions that you make. Your decisions, however small, are too precious to relinquish to others.

How To Stop Failing

Early this year I set a goal for myself to smoothly rise to *pincha mahurasana* in the middle of the room.

The pose is an inversion and requires that you stand on your forearms.

I had a lot of work to do to get to do this pose.

First, I needed to build up to it. Other poses help prepare you for this one.

Then, I needed to intimately understand it. Proper alignment reduces the risk for injury.

I needed to regard my fear with respect. Was I afraid because I was trying something new, or was I afraid because I could fall and hurt my neck or my back?

Was my fear the kind that protects me, or the kind that gets me stuck?

Then I needed to get strong.

I went into the yoga studio every day, and every day gave the pose a try.

I "failed" day after day.

Every day I learned something new.

Sometimes what I learned was subtle. Sometimes it was big.

It was important to distance my arms just right. I needed to pull my elbows in. I had to engage the muscles that wrap around my upper back by hollowing out my armpits. I needed to look up.

I had to engage my core.

Huh. This pose is mostly abs.

A couple of weeks ago I held the pose in the middle of the room, without wall support, and could do it again every day after that.

(I'm still working on the part where I accomplish this "smoothly".)

So, tell me. All those days I couldn't do this pose, was I failing or was I practicing?

And, if I stop failing, won't that mean I never again get to try anything that challenges me?

How Competitive Are You?

Being competitive is the twin of comparing yourself to others.

It insinuates you are spending time looking at what everyone else is doing instead of focusing on what you are doing.

I find this has a tendency to lead me astray.

Being competitive wakes up feelings in me I very rarely feel, like envy, or discouragement, or arrogance.

I want whatever I am working on now to be better than whatever I was busy with a few months ago.

I only compete with myself.

Room For Everyone

In a yoga class, the instant I turn around and notice how bendy the person next to me is, how graceful, how elastic, is the instant I look away from where I am and tune into my ego.

I try to get into her pose instead of into mine, which is the quickest way to get misaligned, possibly hurt.

If instead I focus on what I can do on that day, I respect myself and the path I am on. I accept my good days and bad days.

I want to be better than I was yesterday but often I'm not, and if I push I risk injury but also frustration. I don't want to be harsh and angry with my body. I want to love it, and the first step to that is to accept.

Incidentally, accepting means relaxing, which sometimes means increasing my ability to get into the pose I strive for.

It would be a lie to say I'm not competitive. I feel flashes of it — just like I feel flashes of inexplicable kinship towards strangers, just like I develop irrational crushes, just like I feel rapture, jealousy, elation, resentment and bliss. My feelings come and go and don't get to rule my actions (or the actions of people around me).

If I let a flash of competitiveness overcome me, I shift the way I regard the world. My brain begins to believe there is scarcity and that only one person can be the best.

I prefer to believe there is room for everyone, and that where I am at right now is the exact right place to be.

Driven

Every day I work with people who have an insanely high drive.

These people have a different way of looking at the world.

Rather than discounting something because *"it isn't possible"* they look at it and wonder *"how can this be possible?"*

Rather than saying *"no one has done this, ergo it can't be done"* they think *"just because no one else has done this doesn't mean I can't get it done."*

Instead of declaring *"that's a rule and therefore I can't break it"* they think *"I don't understand why that is a rule and the fact that it's a rule doesn't necessarily mean I have to agree that it makes sense."*

They shake their heads at *"this is how we've always done this."*

People who are driven are audacious, defy logic, and often accomplish incredible things simply because they see possibility where the rest of us see a brick wall.

It would be good for all of us to at least sometimes disbelieve our limitations.

Lack Of Mindfulness

Any time your mind is distracted and not fully engaged in what you are doing is defined as lack of mindfulness.

Some examples:

Talking with someone on the phone while attempting to get other things done.

Talking on the phone and thinking of other things, saying *uh huh, uh huh* but not really listening.

Eating lunch while you are working or doing homework.

Snacking on things while watching TV. (Where did the contents of this whole bag of chips go?)

Any form of multitasking.

Worrying or allowing your brain to fret or wander instead of paying attention to conversations.

Thinking of all the things you need to do or all the errands you need to run or the things you need to get at the supermarket while jogging.

Walking down the street while looking down at your mobile device.

To be more mindful, slow down. Focus on the task at hand. Do one thing at a time.

Put the phone down.

Why "Take A Break"?

"Taking a break" sounds like you are not getting the job done.

Instead, it's an integral part of getting the job done.

It allows you to rest, gain perspective, refresh your viewpoint, approach things with increased clarity, gather your strength and return to battle on a brand new day.

Go ahead. Step away. It will all look better in the morning.

How You Know You Have Become An Adult

You realize that the age you become an adult somehow keeps moving out and that adults don't exist. Everybody is just winging it. (Or maybe that's just me.)

You do what you have to get done. "Being motivated" to do it is irrelevant.

You know that everyone's priority is themselves, not you, that nothing is personal (it's not about you) and that blame does not exist (it's always you).

You have gone from feeling special to the horror of realizing you are not special to understanding you are indeed special but that this does not mean you get special treatment.

You know the world owes you nothing.

You see that "winning" an argument is astoundingly shortsighted.

That there is nothing more important you could be doing with your time than being there for the people who matter to you.

That closing off your heart is worse than death and that it's better to love even if it means you will get hurt a thousand times. And you will.

That you feeling that everyone is better off than you is a story you tell yourself and that it's not even interesting.

The realization that you have less time than you think. And where did it all go, anyway?

That everything you do has consequences, and therefore everything counts. Yes, even that.

That silence is indispensable.

You understand everything is a contradiction — life is painful and unfair, and beautiful, a gift, a curse, a blessing — because everything exists at once.

Indispensable

A friend of mine, let's call her Sandy, was incredibly busy in the office and called her mother to say she could not attend a family trip due to work obligations.

"Why don't you get someone to help you?" her mom asked.

"Because I have to do it. If I don't do it, it doesn't get done right, Mom."

"Oh, Sandy," her mother replied. *"The cemetery is filled with people who considered themselves indispensable."*

How Replaceable Are You?

As it relates to work, I believe I'm objectively good at what I do.

In addition to this, I have carved out a niche for myself that due to my experience, background and perspective is not easy to replicate.

Despite all this I don't delude myself: I am easily replaceable.

This is because to companies there is always more than one way to get something done.

If I stop working for someone and the value I added can't be found they will find another way.

After their goodbye employee lunch and the email wishing me well on my future endeavors, the business will survive without me.

To my mother I am tragically irreplaceable. No one comes close to me.

To varying degrees this applies to the people who love me: my family, Boyfriend, my friends.

They all have (respectively) other family members, other women they might be interested in, other friends, but all those others are not me and as such it would not be the same.

This is something on the top of my mind every time I need to decide where I should be spending the bulk of both my effort and my time.

There will always be another very important project. I am not missing the family reunion.

Has An Intern Ever Been Fired For Being Incompetent?

Of course.

This is because there is a distinction to be made between experience (wisdom gained through what you have done), and competence (possession of skills relevant to what is required of you).

Competence is associated with aptitude but also with common sense, ethical behavior, and an ability to lighten the load for others.

How To Fire Someone

Firing someone can be scary and intimidating.

I mean for the person doing the firing.

The reason I bring this up is because many mistakes are made because the person doing the firing is, without realizing it, coming from a place of fear.

If you are in a situation that causes you stress you're in "fight or flight" mode and treating someone with dignity and respect seems counter to your instincts (that demand at a primal level that you protect yourself).

If you are aware of this you can remind yourself the person you are talking to is under more duress than you; and you can make an effort to not be on the defensive or unnecessarily aggressive.

But I'm getting ahead of myself.

The most important step happens weeks or months before the moment you have to fire someone.

We all need and deserve immediate, clear, direct, regular feedback.

We can't fix what we don't see.

If a manager is providing regular, immediate feedback, when the day comes to fire an employee the conversation does not come as a surprise.

The end of a process is always better than absolute shock.

The next consideration is emotion. The advice I was always given was to not show any but I learned through the years that admitting to feeling terrible makes the situation softer and more human.

Next is a firm, clear, brief, unequivocal explanation as to why the firing is taking place that focuses on the person's performance rather than on who the person is. (*"Deadlines were rarely met"* rather than *"you are irresponsible".*)

If possible, grant the person getting fired the opportunity to determine some of the next steps. For example: *I'm going to write an email with the news of your departure. Could you please review it before I send it out?*

This softens the sense of a sudden and total loss of control.

Be available afterwards (as the employee packs up her desk) and ask how you can help and how she is doing. (*Can we bring you some boxes? Would you like to return after hours to pick up your things?*)

As far as possible, avoid escorting someone out of the building. It ensures things end on a sour note, and they don't have to.

Finally, remember how small the world is. The person you are firing today can be your boss at another job tomorrow.

Who am I?

The Universe is not outside of you.

Look inside yourself:

everything you want you already are.

*— **Rumi***

Misfit

I'm a misfit.

I wanted to be like others and even tried to force-shape myself into what I thought others would like, but the fact is I'm not like them. I'm like me.

At first I spent a whole lot of time trying to figure out how not to be a misfit, and how to hide what made me different.

One day I decided it would be easier to invest that time in learning more about myself.

Who am I? What is it that makes me happy? Fulfilled? What gives me a sense of purpose? What exactly makes me not like you?

These answers are not fixed. They evolve. Exploring them has again and again revealed my life and my career path (because those two are not separate things).

The answers to these questions are stepping stones to what will motivate me, what will give my life meaning, what will make me successful.

No one in the world has the answers to these questions but you.

Not even people who adore you and shower you with well intentioned advice. You need to figure this out on your own.

Start here.

Implausible You

Here are a few hypothetical questions designed to reveal something to you about your own life:

There is a secret goal you'd like to set but you don't because it's completely implausible. What is it? What if I told you it was instead viable?

If you could plan a perfect day, what would it look like?

What about a perfect life?

Who would you be if you weren't you?

Who would you be if what others thought or expected didn't matter? How would your choices be different if they were made only for you?

Make an exhaustive list of everything you are afraid of. (You can add to this list at any time.) Assume none of the things on this list will ever happen. How does that change your plans?

Make an exhaustive list of everything that is stopping you, limiting you, hindering you, blocking you. (You can add to this list at any time.) What if you forced your brain to convince you none of these things were real? Could you write down next to every one a credible argument disbelieving it? (This is really, really difficult, and really, really good because it teaches your brain to see things differently.)

If you didn't do what you do, what would you do?

If you could learn the answer to any one question, what would you ask?

How would your life change if you won the lottery?

How would your life change if you knew the date of your death?

If you could be really good at something you currently don't know how to do, what would it be?

If you could change the world, how would you?

If you were a superhero (and you are), what would be your superpower?

If you could create a place to hide, what would it look like? Where would it be?

If all your wishes came true, what would you do next?

In other words, you have everything you wanted. Now what?

Serendipity

Serendipity is one of my favorite words, and I am absolutely fascinated by what it means.

First of all, (to me) the word is onomatopoeic. "Serendipity" somehow sounds like its definition: languid at first, with a delicious, mischievous, unexpected burst at the tail end of it.

Its etymology is unique. It doesn't come from the Greek or Latin. Horace Walpole coined the term because he felt it was a quality possessed by the protagonists of the story *The Three Princes of Serendip*.

Walpole noted that:

"As their highnesses traveled, they were always making discoveries, by accident and sagacity, of things which they were not in quest of."

I am convinced that the way we lead our lives — overplanning, overbooking, developing hard lists of goals and objectives, cramming our schedules full, placing so much importance on being very, very busy, and never looking up from our devices — is tragically shrinking our chances of encountering serendipity.

I also believe that serendipity is one of the best parts of life.

This is why I need to be more open to the wonders I have inadvertently closed myself off to due to having my calendar booked with a meeting every half hour.

Luck and serendipity are very different. Luck is good fortune. Serendipity is *finding something wonderful that you didn't know you were looking for.*

I came across an article published in The New York Times (January 2, 2016) titled *"How to cultivate the art of serendipity".*

The writer, Pagan Kennedy, notes that many inventions were stumbled upon by accident, which led to her wondering if serendipity could be fostered, nurtured, architected.

She points out that Walpole (the man who coined the word) originally proposed it as a talent for a particular kind of detective work.

This means serendipity isn't an accident.

Serendipity is a skill.

A University of Missouri information scientist named Sandra Erdelez began a study to find out how people created (or didn't) their own serendipity.

(As I write this I am freaking out at how wonderful this information is. Phew.)

Her data shows three groups of people:

Those who don't experience serendipity. They (and this is a direct quote) *"tend to stick to their to-do lists."*

People who sometimes experience serendipity.

And what she calls the "super-encounterers" — who reported finding serendipity everywhere.

You become a super-encounterer, according to Dr. Erdelez, in part because you believe you are.

To me this means feeling lost might be the best thing that ever happened to you (and to me).

Open your eyes. Open your heart. Set goals, but learn to recognize unexpected opportunity.

Life has in store for you things more wonderful than anything you could anticipate, but you will not see it if you don't believe it.

What Is The Difference Between Truth And Fact?

Facts are the pieces of a large puzzle.

As they click into place they reveal a final image.

The final image is the truth.

Except the puzzle pieces of life are often designed to fit perfectly in more than one way.

We are each convinced that the image we see is the only one to result from the correct assembly of the puzzle pieces.

This is not always the case.

How Can I Set Career Goals If I Don't Know What I Want To Do?

I have never felt sure about what I want to be doing.

Even when I think I know what I want, I realize later I really didn't.

(It feels like this: *how come I have everything I want and I'm still not happy?*)

How can I claim to know what I want when the future is full of variables I have no insight into?

Embracing that (gasp!) I don't know what I want leaves me open and receptive to possibilities that exceed my own inadvertently cautious dreams.

It makes me resilient to change.

Even if you don't know what you want to do next, there is still a lot you can do:

Between an easy job and one where you can learn more, pick learning more.

Between better pay or learning more, pick learning more.

Between doing what you already know how to do or doing things you've never done before, pick what you've never done before.

People will often be convinced you can do something you don't think you can do. Believe them.

People will often underestimate you, be certain you can't possibly do something you are sure you can. Don't listen to them.

Every time you say you will do something, follow through. In business, "reliable" is more valuable that you'd ever think.

Notice what comes easily to you that does not come easily to others. This is the initial clue to how you can begin to position yourself so that no one can compete.

It's tempting to put your head down and focus on your own work. Never lose sight of how what you do fits into the big picture. Losing the big picture perspective might feel like focus. It isn't.

You need others. This doesn't mean politics. This means allies, accomplices, teams. Find them.

If you do all these things there will come a day where you will look back and feel incredulous at how far you've come, at how many things you have that make you happy that you didn't even know you wanted.

How To Be Limitless

I was having coffee with a friend. She was telling me she was stuck. There was no way she could get a job. Not in her current condition.

To which I eloquently said *"Huh?".*

"Dushka," she said. *"I'm three months pregnant."*

"But, how on Earth would that stop you from getting a job? Go prepare, give the best interview you possibly can and see how far you can get."

A month later she had a job. She then got paid through maternity leave, after which she returned to work.

I catch myself thinking like her all the time, convinced that there is so much out there I can't do. Because, it wouldn't work. Because others have tried it. Because it seems crazy.

That's when I remind myself I'm limitless.

Am I saying limits don't exist? Am I telling you that forces such as gravity are only an illusion?

Of course not. What I'm saying is there are so many things out there that limit you that it's doubly important for you to pay no heed to the ones that exist only in your mind.

In your mind, be limitless.

Don't allow your own assumptions to stop you. The whole world is ready to do that for you.

Which reminds me of the comic strip Garfield. Jon, his owner, finds both Odie and Garfield high up in a tree. *"But Odie,"* Jon says. *"Dogs can't climb trees."*

To which Garfield says, *"It's amazing what one can accomplish when one doesn't know what one can't do."*

Do We Need Help From Others?

I have no sense of direction.

I don't mean this in a quirky, funny way. I mean it in an impairing way. I don't know where I am and it makes things that are easy for you very difficult for me.

I give myself loads of extra time to get anywhere because I know I will wander around aimlessly for some time.

I was recently trying to get to an important business meeting and I couldn't find the address.

After 45 minutes of walking back and forth within a few blocks I was so frustrated I was ready to call and cancel. Throw in the towel. Give up.

I stood alone on the sidewalk and felt like crying.

How can I be so inadequate?

As a last resort I stopped a stranger. *"Would you happen to know where street number 317 is?"*

She looks up at me, glances at the screen on my phone.

"Your map says it's a block down that way. Here, I will take you."

"Here, I will take you" sounds to me like someone is gently tossing rose petals over my head.

I check her back to see if her scapula sprout wings.

She walks lightly beside me all the way to the entrance of the building I am looking for.

"Good luck!" She waves and walks off.

I stand there considering two things: that I can't really get anything done without the help of others, and that more often than not what I'm looking for is just around the corner.

Just Ask. No, Really.

Many things I want are available to me — if only I would ask for them.

I don't know why, but I forget that I can ask.

Or, I tell myself that I shouldn't. Because, how scary. Or uncomfort- able. Or inappropriate. Or implausible.

Because I should get it without having to ask for it.

(*Dushka. Get over yourself. This makes no sense.*)

It's hard to ask. I don't know why.

Would you like a chance to be involved in a specific project at work? Do you think it's time you were considered for another position within your company, for a raise, for a promotion? Do you think it would be fun or different to work in another team?

Or, beyond work and what we read about on LinkedIn, how about seeing your significant other more? Or less? Do you want a date night? A time alone night?

Do you want to approach that really hot girl (or guy)?

Do you dream of taking a weekend trip with a friend you haven't seen in a while? Or even catching up over coffee?

I need to ask for what I want more often.

To stop myself less often.

Because at worst the person I am asking will say no, which would leave me in exactly the same place I already am (a place I am absolutely guaranteed to stay at if I don't ask).

And at best, you get better at anything you practice.

I want to be an expert at asking for what I want.

Don't Miss Everything

I went to a really difficult yoga class today. It wasn't about elaborate poses. It was about bringing your full intention to the poses you would consider the most simple.

Take Mountain Pose.

It looks like you're just standing, but done right every muscle in your body should be active, alive.

It's tragically easy to let your feet relax, a hip jut out, your back slump. All it takes is an instant of distraction.

If you get distracted, your mind wanders. If your mind wanders, the effect yoga has on you — the centering, the calming, the grounding, the muscle strength, the fitness — is impacted.

Which of course applies to everything.

How many times am I getting ready to go to work and forget — with the chatter in my head, the messages in my phone, the running checklist of things I have to do — if I brushed my teeth or not?

How often do we go to work to collect a paycheck in return for minimal effort?

How often do we feel our jobs bore us, that we are disengaged, unfulfilled, feel no passion, that we can do everything "with a hand tied behind our back"?

Instead of these feelings scaring us away they become our prison.

God forbid we end up somewhere that requires effort.

And what about our relationships? Are we there when our family arrives, or do we sit down on the couch, our attention on surfing through channels of bad TV we don't even want to watch instead of each other?

Letting our brain switch to automatic mode is easy and tempting but instead of refreshing us or providing solace it's sucking the vitality out of us.

Sleepwalking through life is an epidemic.

We think we are so shrewd, getting away with coasting, but what we are doing with each hour we are not engaged is what we are doing with our life.

Then we wonder: *Why do I feel lost? Why can't I find my passion? Why is opportunity so scarce? Why don't I know where I'm going or what I want to do next?*

How on Earth did I end up here?

Which is akin to wondering why we have trouble following a class we seldom bother to attend.

It is so very difficult to be present in Mountain Pose. Sometimes I tell myself so fervently that I need to pay attention that I realize trying to pay attention has distracted me.

Often I am convinced I am absolutely focused, standing straight, feet rooted, and the teacher asks if our core is engaged and I realize mine is not. And once it is, I have completely forgotten about firing up my legs.

Life is the arduous exercise of remaining present.

The price of not making this effort is to miss everything.

How Can I Stop Being Average?

How many times have you seen someone work harder than anyone else and still be unable to get ahead?

To defy being average you have to change the game.

You have to "position yourself or be positioned": offer something different so that rather than competing with others you are in a place of your own design where no one else can do what you do.

It's about hard work, sure, but it's about getting people to see you a certain way.

By way of example, Mahatma Gandhi created "nonviolent resistance" and will forever stand in a category of his own creation.

Not everyone can make a dent of that magnitude in the world but everyone can make a mark in their own world by developing a clear vision of who they are, the unique problem they solve, and a point of view.

There is a problem out there that has not been articulated that only you can define and solve.

The Man In The Yellow Shirt

Close to where I live there is a hill.

At the foot of it there is a labyrinth.

A few times a month I come upon this labyrinth and have been noticing how its outlines are beginning to fade.

It made me think how the world tends towards chaos rather than order and how some day soon there would be no trace of it.

Except today I saw a man in a yellow shirt.

He was dragging his feet along the path.

I watched him kick into place every rock.

I walked around the hill and came back and he was still at it.

We can complain or lament or have wistful thoughts or we can get up early on a Saturday morning and put things back where they belong.

How Can I Be More Powerful?

I was recently made an offer for a big job that terrified me. What if I accepted it and had no time left for myself? When would I write? And, what if I messed it up? What if I couldn't do it and everyone found out I was not good enough?

I loved the work that I was doing. I found it interesting, and was learning so much.

What's it going to be, Dushka? Is fear going to win, or the fact that you love what you are doing?

Fear shrinks my world. Love is expansive and brave. Whenever I identify that I can let fear guide me or love guide me, I try my darndest to choose love.

Many years ago I was dating a guy who wanted me, except when he didn't. I spent nights awake wondering why his interest was so volatile. What could I do to keep him with me? What was it about me that he found so unconvincing?

I finally realized that my power did not lie in decoding him or in getting him to do anything differently but rather in turning the questions towards me. Why did I choose a love that was fickle? What was it about me that made me feel that this kind of relationship would do?

Whenever I am in a situation where I feel helpless and wish I could refocus or change somebody else I remind myself that I'm entirely missing the point. This is not about anyone other than me. This reframing places me in the most frightening of places: in the driver's seat. From here, I get to decide.

I do this same thing when I find myself waiting for others to make the decision that will propel me into action. Am I asking for permission? Am I expecting advice? Do I want someone to tell me what to do? Again, Dushka. This is your life. The boss is you. Get comfortable with the reins in your hands.

In order to not risk offending others, in order to be liked by as many people as possible, I used to lie a lot. I lied about why I didn't ever go to parties — or worse, ended up going despite wanting with all my heart to stay home instead. Telling the truth revealed who I really was. This automatically selected the people who liked me for me. Do you know what was harder still? It forced me to accept that not everyone was going to like me.

I want to but resist doing things in an attempt to get approval. It's not my job to get you to approve of me. It's my job to like myself. At the end of the day you get to go home and I'm the one who has to live with me.

I could moan all day about all the things I wanted that I didn't have, all of the perceived riches others rejoiced in that I had no access to — or I could focus on what I had been given. This word — gratitude — is so overused it sounds corny. Set aside how it sounds and let me tell you: gratitude is the key to happiness. It refocuses your attention on what matters and expands your heart.

Gratitude is the very definition of power. You are nearly invincible if you want for nothing and feel overwhelmed at your own good fortune.

What To Do When You Don't Know What To Do

Imagine you are in a car driving down the highway. Suddenly, a large, thick tarp flies onto your windshield, completely blocking your vision.

What do you do?

As carefully and as quickly as possible, you pull over. You cannot keep driving down the highway if you can't see.

If you don't know what to do, pull over. Rest. Wait. Stretch your legs. Clear your windshield.

If you don't know what to do, do nothing. Really. Nothing.

You cannot — should not — keep going if you can't see.

The Ultimate Productivity Tool

I had all these self-soothing mechanisms and for so long I was convinced they really helped me.

But really, they only made me want them more.

I made general lists. Kitchen lists. Shopping lists. To do lists.

I made lists even though I knew by heart their content just to quiet the rattling in my brain of all the things I needed to get done.

I bought notebooks to put my lists in.

I had a list of list categories.

I finally realized I don't need more lists. I know what I need to do.

I need to breathe.

That is my ultimate productivity tool.

Stacking Improbable Things

My best friend lives in Costa Rica, tends to a vegetable garden in the back of her house, and makes a successful living by giving online courses on health and wellness.

She did not know what she would do when she was little because the internet (and therefore online courses) did not exist.

She loved gardening and food and always dreamed of living in a remote location in the middle of the jungle.

How would these things ever come together into a semblance of a way of life?

There is nothing to "find". You *create* passion by stacking the often improbable things that you love and seeing what you come up with.

How To Be More Creative

To become more creative, I had to begin by reconsidering the way I regarded concepts like "procrastination", "efficiency" and "being busy".

I believed procrastination was a bad thing.

I'd make a to do list and blow through it.

Rather than leaving things for later I took pleasure in ticking things off.

Done. Done.

Aaaand, done.

I have discovered that my compulsion with checking things off a list without delay precludes me from considering something from a different angle, solving it in a new way, or even avoiding it altogether.

Expediency sacrifices creativity.

I placed a high value on efficiency.

In an effort to make my life simpler I noticed I had over-stripped it of complications.

Life, art, beauty and pleasure all hide in the complex web that is inconvenience.

Cooking quickly is often necessary. But what about preparing an elaborate meal because it's a joy?

The decision to add sprinkles to a cake, which might mean having to go buy them. Are sprinkles ever a requirement? Not really. Are sprinkles awesome? Yes. Yes they are.

What about spending a weekend putting together a perfect costume because dressing up to go roller skating in elaborate 70s outfits is laughter inducing?

What about lying flat on your back for years to paint the ceiling of the Sistine Chapel?

I felt better about myself when my schedule was packed.

As if "busy" was the equivalent of *"I am doing well"*, or the even more preposterous *"I matter. I am very very important"*.

What if instead of "busy" I made space for wandering? Gave myself time to be idle?

Less to do is the window for creativity, for serendipity, and yes. Even for sanity.

What To Do If You Are Feeling Overwhelmed

I often feel overwhelmed.

I am regularly under the impression that I have more to do than time to do it and before I know it I am reminding myself that I need to take deep breaths.

When I feel this way I resort to making lists. I write down everything I need to do so I can look at it.

Sometimes I glance at the list and recognize my feelings are valid.

But just as often I look at the list and realize my load is reasonable.

From this I conclude that feeling overwhelmed is not necessarily related to what is happening outside of me: I can feel overwhelmed and have nearly nothing to do.

(This is a lesson I encounter again and again. The solution is within, not out there.)

The last time I felt really overwhelmed it was around 3:00 p.m. and I needed to get quite a bit done before bedtime. I was frazzled and tired and I looked at my desk and looked at my couch and looked at my desk and looked at my couch and in a move completely out of character I walked over the the sofa, lay down and took a nap.

I slept for four hours.

You might assume this course of action led to disaster. Instead, when I woke up I felt rested, clear headed, lucid. I worked through everything I needed to do before 11:00 p.m.

It's so common to declare *"I am so busy I don't have time to sleep"*. I prefer *"I am so busy I don't have time to not sleep"*.

Sleep is my antidote to feeling overwhelmed.

For The Heck Of It

Right after I quit my job I enrolled in a yoga teacher training to become a certified yoga teacher. I did this with no intention to ever teach yoga.

When I finished this course and got my certification I enrolled in another course for yoga therapeutics, to assist students into proper alignment. Still, no intention to ever teach.

Friends often ask why I did all this work if I did not intend to apply it.

I decided that not everywhere I went needed to come with a destination, and that the notion of doing things for the heck of it made more life-sense to me.

If I approach everything thinking it all must have a purpose, everything I set out to do becomes more intimidating than it needs to be.

I make it harder for myself to experience new things.

I want to study what interests me to understand it better, and it doesn't matter if what I learn is ever "put to use". Learning is its own reward, and the same holds true for everything.

Curiosity reveals new paths that are meant to be explored. (Maybe it killed the cat. But I am not a cat.)

I remained in a job for years because the decision to leave seemed terrifying and final. I didn't walk away until it dawned on me that if I did, I could return any time.

When we're all tangled up in one it's hard to see, but decisions are seldom as big as we make them out to be.

Everything changes anyway.

Take Quora. I spend time on that site because I like it. So many people ask me where I'm going with it or what it's all for.

I have no answers for either of these questions but can tell you my activity there has so far resulted in five books.

If I had set out to write five books, I would not have been able to do it.

Answering questions on a site sounds like play. Writing a series of books sounds daunting.

Regardless of how seriously we take things, the truth is life is more than anything the art of going nowhere.

Pretty much everything I do is for the heck of it, and I would recommend this approach to anyone who has ever felt stuck.

Why Am I Always Running Out Of Time?

I find I invariably have less of whatever it is I chase.

In my experience the sense that I'm running out of time is not alleviated by prioritizing, scheduling or organizing. All these things play into the illusion that time is scarce and that I will never, ever have enough to do all the things I want. This can only contribute to making things worse.

When I slow down, time slows down.

I practice doing one thing at a time, with my full attention, and tell myself my day is as long as I want it to be.

I realize time needs a reference, and the reference is me.

This is how I seem to have time for everything.

How Do I Stop Wasting Time?

Too often in my life I have experienced wonderful things thanks to other things I have done that were not so wonderful.

I would never be in the relationship I am now if it wasn't for the ones that didn't go so well. I would not be doing the fun work I'm doing today if I hadn't learned all the things I did in the jobs where I was often unhappy.

Life keeps reminding me that there is no such thing as a waste of time.

Work Less

Imagine for a moment that I am aboard a big ship in the middle of the ocean. I fall off this ship into the choppy waters below.

I'm a decent swimmer, despite of which I begin to thrash. I thrash because I'm terrified. I fell off a ship, cannot see land, and don't know what else is in the water.

I am unlikely to make it if I keep thrashing. Thrashing is ineffective and expends energy that I should be trying to conserve. I could be swimming way more slowly, in a more coordinated way. I could even be mostly floating.

Which is to say maximum effort does not equal maximum results.

My life sometimes feels like I have fallen off a ship in the middle of the ocean, and I indeed thrash around a lot. In small and big ways I work harder than I need to.

I wake up with a tense jaw because I have been gnashing my teeth while I sleep. At the end of the day I frequently have pain in my shoulders even when I don't remember using them for anything.

I clench my jaws when I hold imaginary arguments with people.

Imaginary arguments. About things that haven't happened.

Sometimes it takes me twenty sentences to explain what I could tell you in six and I fret about things I have no control over — at least not through fretting.

I intensely partake in wishful thinking instead of preparedness and mistrust people to do what they tell me they are going to do.

Trusting is liberating.

I have resolved to be more vigilant about the ways I work harder than I have to, not so much because I want to work less but because I need every ounce of power applied to places where my effort is more likely to count.

How Do I Stop Comparing Myself To Others?

The first time I went to a yoga class I did not want to go back.

Everyone was better than me.

Everyone was bendier and more graceful. I couldn't even touch my toes.

The more I looked at others the worse I did.

Not only because I felt increasingly inadequate but because I forced myself into the poses they could do and I couldn't.

Ouch.

I found that if I focused on myself I made a lot more progress.

I had to begin by accepting exactly where I was.

I had to determine what worked for me, regardless of what worked for everyone else.

I stopped comparing myself to others when I understood that every second spent looking at someone else would be better spent working on myself.

What Is The Difference Between Who You Are And What You Do?

If you are a company, who you are is your corporate image and what you do is a list and description of your products.

This notion is very simple if you are a person but we get tripped up because we entangle who we are into what we do.

This leads to a very common and completely unnecessary identity crisis.

Someone may ask me to introduce myself and I might say *"Hello, I'm Dushka. I'm Vice President of Corporate Communications at Zendesk."*

But then, when I resign from this job, what will be left of me?

Look at your life. You might be an executive, a mom, a housewife, a runner, a swimmer, a teacher, a coach.

Remove what you do.

What remains?

Who are you?

Your identity (also referred to as your "brand") is built around the answer to this question.

If you are a CEO and leave your job who are you? If you are a mom and your kids grow up and leave who are you? If you are a wife and get a divorce who are you?

You can (and often do) remove, switch out, outgrow, evolve or develop what you do to realize in an act of glorious recognition that who you are remains. It's strong. It's intact. Despite your terror, it's still here, glistening in the sun.

You are not what you do. You are way more than that.

Please Don't Call It Personal Branding

In an ironic twist of fate, I will begin by admitting that the term "personal brand" makes me cringe.

It's not just that it sounds ego-driven. It's that calling it that means that we're missing something essential.

Wanting a personal brand assumes we need a brand to shape us. Really, it's the other way around. We design, give shape to, determine a brand.

A "brand" was originally intended to anthropomorphize a company by giving it a personality, in order to make it unique, to tell it apart from others. You, a human being, already have a personality. You come equipped with it at birth. You don't want to develop a brand.

What you want is to identify the brand (if we must call it that) that you already have.

To do this, you have a single question to answer. What is it that you do that would be of service? To rephrase, what do you have to give to others? Can you articulate that?

Think beyond your current job and even your next one. Think more along the lines of what matters to you, what you love, what you'd like to leave behind.

In the words of David Brooks, who wrote the brilliant article "The Moral Bucket List", *"Consider less your résumé virtues, and think about your eulogy virtues."* First because these are what most faithfully make you you — but also because this is what both individuals and the world need the most.

Focusing on what we want to leave behind is also the antidote to our increasing terror of becoming irrelevant.

"Relevance" means "connected," as in "connected to the matter at hand." It comes from the Latin "to lift, to raise up." Relevance has to do with real life. Our secret, regular acts of heroism make us relevant. Our relevance is in being human, in loving, in being a part of our family, our community, in showing up. In other words, you don't really need to "struggle to remain" something you already are.

Much like the concept of "a personal brand", "struggling to remain relevant" is a false premise: it misleads you into assuming "relevance" is defined by clicks or likes.

The only way to escape this soul sapping like-chasing pathology is to operate from a place of conviction (I would say "authenticity" but feel we've beaten that one beyond recognition).

Put simply, it means you should do and say things because they are important to you.

"Do what you love" has become tired and sappy but look at it. It's your life force. It's tied to competence, productivity, even relevance. When you love doing something, you want to do it a lot. You are — almost accidentally — practicing, improving, exploring, learning, expanding, all the time. There is no way to remain competitive against someone who loves what you slog through.

This practice of, in a sense, moving towards a sense of purpose through doing what matters to you, what makes you fulfilled in this moment, even if you are doing so inch by inch, by trial and error, will unequivocally identify you. It will also make companies that you work for better for having you — and this energy you bring — be a part of them.

Who you are and what you do are meant to be cohesive. What you do all those hours that you are in the office amounts, in effect, to your life's work. To quote Annie Dillard, *"How you spend your days is, of course, how you spend your life."*

I don't mean to imply that this is easy. It will, in fact, be the hardest, most important thing you do; an ever-evolving series of experiments that will take the rest of your life. But you will be creating something that feeds you, that provides a clear direction towards your own evolution (and priorities), and that (hopefully) leaves things better than how you found them.

It's about so much more than "managing your brand." It's how we each choose to contribute to make ourselves better, in turn making the world a better place.

Sunday Blues

I suffered from Sunday blues, which I would define as a weight on my chest and low grade anxiety related to what awaited me the following day (even if on the following day it wasn't even so bad).

My first (quite effective) remedy was to organize an early evening out with a small group of friends on Sunday afternoons.

This ensured that instead of spending Sunday preparing for Monday I spent the day enjoying what was left of the weekend.

It made my weekends feel longer and gave me a chance to catch up with people I wanted to see.

After some time I decided my Sunday tradition of going out with friends was, rather than a solution, a way to cover the real problem.

Dreading a seventh of your life is no way to live.

What I really needed was a permanent cure. A solid plan.

I needed to create a life I would not dread going back to.

How Should I Define Priorities?

You know what makes prioritization incredibly difficult?

Me.

To prioritize, the first thing I do is check my ego. I associate being busy with feeling important, so make myself busy with work that isn't real.

I also deceive myself into considering the things I am keeping myself busy with are more significant than they really are. If I am very, very busy doing mission critical things, then that must mean I matter, right?

Next I spend some time alone, maybe on a long walk. I go somewhere with a view so I can see the city where I live from above. I take stock of my life. Who do I want to be? What do I want to leave behind?

With this on my mind I find a place to sit and write down all the things I fill my days with. This fresh, new sense of perspective makes it easier for me to distinguish what is important from what is not.

This is how I create a "things not to do" list. Prioritization is a constant, daily, often ruthless practice. I have to relentlessly remind myself what my priorities are and what things I spend a lot of time on that really don't ever need to get done. Not ever.

On that "things not to do" list, I add *"I know you want to, and I know it's hard, but don't listen to others"*. This is because it's easy for me to allow other people to tell me what is urgent and critical and requires my immediate, undivided attention.

No matter how much I want to please them, they do not decide my priorities. Only I can do that.

This is my time. My time is my life. This is all I have.

Does Being Lost Mean You Cannot Find Your Way Back, Or That You Cannot Find The Way To Your Destination?

Being lost means you don't know where you are. You don't know how to get where you are going. You don't know how to retrace your steps. It means you missed the way.

Lost can also mean you have no faith or hope or that you were once in firm possession of something you suddenly don't have or can no longer find.

Lost can refer to waste, like a glittering opportunity you didn't pay attention to or time you didn't put to good use.

It also refers to something that could have been yours, to something you could have won but didn't.

It means astray, irretrievable, squandered or forgotten. It means misspent.

But you know what it also means? It means a clean slate for you to start over. It means a road not traveled that you can explore. It means adventure. It means open to serendipity.

It means you are about to learn something about the world and about yourself.

If you can begin again then nothing is lost — and you can always, always begin again.

Leaving Your Job

What you seek is seeking you.

— Rumi

The Wrong Job

While I ask myself if I am or am not in the wrong job, my body already knows and is trying to tell me.

Here is what that feels like:

Sunday dread. Sunday should be relaxing and peaceful. If I feel like someone threw a dark cloak over me just because I have to go into work the next day, it's safe to assume I might be in the wrong job.

It irritates me when someone asks me what I do. Talking about what I do should make me enthusiastic. I share what makes me proud. Why then am I feeling miffed and resentful, overdrawn?

Getting myself to work is a monumental effort. I can't get up in the morning. I can't seem to function without more caffeine. I keep forgetting things.

Work makes me sad. There is a sense of constriction, tightness. This is not normal. Work is not supposed to feel like a sentence, like a prison, like I am trapped.

At work I feel like a different person. I am stressed, I am anxious, I am short. I snap at people. I come across as rude.

The only good reason I am still here is the money. I am not suggesting money doesn't matter. But money should never be at the center of my decisions, in particular because the notion that I can't be both happy and well paid is a fabrication. I remind myself of that so that I never live a life trapped by lies of my own creation.

I count the minutes. I wonder if the clock has stopped. Every time I stare at it and wonder when the day is going to end I remind myself that my time at work is my life. My life is ticking away. It's my life I am wishing went by faster.

I get consistently bad feedback. This is an indication that my talent is somewhere else and that I have to go find a place where I am useful.

I get feedback that demands I be different rather than better. If what I am being told to do stretches me, challenges me, demands more of me, that is different from feeling like my work requires that I be somebody else.

Setting all this aside, there is a single, quick, infallible way to tell if I am in the wrong job: **I am not learning anything new.**

Learning is a key ingredient to happiness: it is stimulating, it is renovating, and is the antidote to boredom and stagnation.

If I am not learning anything new I am dulling my senses and stifling my future. It's time to go find a place that reinvigorates me.

Here And Now

I have a dress in my closet that I never use. I recently placed it in a suitcase and took it on a trip.

Somewhere in the inner workings of my brain I decided that in another location I'd be a person interested in wearing it.

Here is what I learned: if I don't want to wear it here and now, chances are I won't want to wear it some other time in some other place.

I feel similarly about things I do or don't want to do. If that activity is something I wish I could be doing right now, chances are I will want to do it later.

If I don't feel like doing it right now, I won't feel like doing it in the future, even if I tell myself I could or should.

Why It's Hard To Leave

Here are some of the reasons why it was hard for me to quit my job:

Because work has always been the framework for my life. I set the alarm to get up early, go into work and organize everything else around the time I have to be in the office. Without a job, how do I structure my life?

Because work has always been a part of my identity. It is very easy to confuse what I do with who I am. What we do is part of what defines us, but I am more than just what I do, and so are you.

Because I set out to do something. When I initially take a job, I have expectations for what it's going to be like and what I am going to accomplish. I get caught up in the discrepancy between what I expect and what it actually is; between what I think I will accomplish and what I actually do. If only I could do this one more thing. It takes me a while to realize this is my ego talking. I can't let my ego be the voice that runs my life.

Because I believe in facing a challenge. If only I had more time, I could improve this. I believe that whatever challenge I am faced with will continue to show up in my life until I fully address it. I tend to stick out difficult situations because I know that the lesson they bring will serve me forever.

Because I don't know what I want to do next, and I want a guarantee that if I quit I will be safe. The job I have now is, for better or worse, what I know. There is a lot of comfort in all the things I already know I can do — even in all the things I already know I can't do. What comes after is unknown, and therefore scary.

The fact is there are no guarantees, and we are never safe.

On the day I finally decided to leave I wasn't particularly unhappy or irritated with anything at work.

It was that I felt a strong pull towards things I really wanted to do that I would never have the time for with a full time job.

The most viable way to quit a comfortable, safe place is to move towards something wonderful, rather than leaving a place because you are unhappy.

Not Disloyal

Whenever I thought about leaving my (first) job I always imagined it would be ugly.

Leaving felt underhanded, illicit, disloyal and a bit like breaking up.

Why would I leave unless something was making me feel wronged or unhappy?

The truth is leaving is always appropriate.

It's the natural thing to do.

You leave because you need to go do something different, and you can always, always do so on good terms.

Leaving a job well will serve you for the rest of your career.

Once you are clear on your next steps you can openly talk to your managers and mentors about what you are thinking so they are part of the process and there are no surprises.

This way you don't leave anyone in a bind.

You can give more than two weeks notice to be a part of transition plans, perhaps help train your replacement.

You can leave behind suggestions on how or what to improve.

You can make friends. *"I see you as more than a coworker. You are my friend and I would like us to stay in touch."*

This is true networking: collecting people that you have enjoyed working with and remaining connected is much more powerful than handing a stranger a flimsy business card at a networking event.

As far as possible avoid leaving a job on bad terms. Be a builder. Create bridges. Leave doors open. Go out of your way to do the right thing.

People will remember.

Moving Towards Something

When I am in a job I find vexing or difficult, I tell myself that every obstacle or frustration has presented itself to teach me something.

Do I need to look at problems differently? Do I need to learn how to be more patient? Do I need to figure out how to work better with others? Should I listen more?

I know it's time to leave when I am being pulled to do something I am excited about, attracted by my future rather than running away from the place where I am at.

The right time to leave is when I come across the chance to do something I really want to do, unrelated to my current job satisfaction.

The Life You Imagine

Many people are stuck because they cannot escape what is immediate and urgent in their lives and are therefore unable to set the foundation for a better future.

If they could, they would not let what is urgent take precedence over what is important.

They would get out there and do as much as possible to set themselves up for radical improvement: a volunteer opportunity and perhaps additional education.

An unfulfilling, dead-end job deludes people into feeling it's their lives that are unfulfilling and a dead end.

We all deserve the promise to ourselves that we can make things better.

We have one life to live, and therefore it would be irresponsible not to.

"Go confidently in the direction of your dreams," commanded Thoreau. *"Live the life you have imagined."*

Distress Tolerance

Have you heard about the notion of "distress tolerance"?

Say I have a bad day at work. I feel angry.

If I have high distress tolerance I recognize that a bad day is a part of life. I see that everything has an ebb and a flow and that this anger is likely to pass. As such, my psyche determines that, while upsetting, I am not in the presence of a catastrophe.

If I have low distress tolerance my whole system is screaming at me to get out. Get out, get out, this is horrible. This is the end. What are you going to do? Will you ever work again? Get your shit together.

This instant fight or flight response forces me to process a bad day as if the loss were total.

It's a faulty, too sensitive survival skill, a constant state of high alert that distracts you from the fact that it is simply not necessary to process everything as cataclysmic.

The flawed logic is that being on instant high alert "prepares me for a crisis." It does not. It's exhausting and deeply painful and recognizing that calamity is not permanent does not make you vulnerable. It makes you suffer less.

Make Space

A few weeks ago I walked into the yoga studio and greeted the office manager. *"Dushka!" She said. "I'm so glad I get to say goodbye in person! Monday is my last day!"*

"Oh," I said. *"Where are you going?"*

"I have no idea," she said. *"But when my day is full I find it hard to see. If I leave my job and clear my schedule and clear my head I make the necessary space for something new to present itself."*

While I fully realize this can be frightening and possibly financially risky, there are ways to mitigate the risk.

The logic that new things don't have space if everything is full makes perfect sense to me.

A Prison, Imagined

I felt trapped in my job.

Here is what I felt trapped by:

A good salary and the sense that I could not live without it.

A feeling that I could never save what I would consider to be "enough". Over the years the number kept moving out.

I felt distress at the thought of leaving my team.

I feared that without the structure of a job I would condemn myself to depression; that I wouldn't know what to do with myself all day and would end up spending my days on the couch watching TV and doing nothing.

This terrified me.

Here is what I very, very slowly learned:

That almost every time I tell myself I'm trapped, it's a fabrication. A prison that exists only in my mind.

To put it in other words, all the thoughts that convince me I am trapped can be inverted to show me I am not.

Like this, look:

There is more than one job where I can make a good salary, and more than one way to make a good salary.

I have enough.

My team is comprised of intelligent adults who don't need me.

If the best that I can do for my team is offer them a trapped, stressed, disengaged version of me, they are better off without me.

I have many interests to pursue and cannot only keep myself busy, I need as much time as I can get to do all the things I need to do.

Rather than feel stuck, I began to plan what my next step would be and what I would need to get me there.

Bonus tip:

Huge changes can be paralyzing due to their sheer enormity. Small changes add up fast, are incredibly effective and get you out of your imaginary prison.

My plan was simple: working as a freelancer rather than a full time employee.

With the money I finance all the things that interest me.

I am not saying this is easy.

I am saying it's possible.

And once your brain moves from "I'm trapped" to "it's possible", you are no longer trapped.

Work For Yourself

I quit a good, well paid, high level corporate job three years ago.

I felt listless, and like I could do my job with a hand tied behind my back.

I wasn't bored. I felt like the colors inside of me had been stripped out.

I felt that there were things I really, deeply wanted to do and recognized in a flash of insight that "the right time" to do them would never come.

It would never be the right time to walk away from a perfectly good job.

When I quit I immediately — within days — felt a rush of life pour back into me. I felt inspired and happy and full instead of angsty and restless and stressed and running on empty.

Boyfriend warned me that after 20 years in a fast paced, competitive, demanding environment being suddenly unemployed might result in an internal crisis I might have to adjust to.

Instead I took to loitering like a fish to water.

I learned a lesson that astounds me: that the secret of happiness, success and creativity is in having chunks of time with nothing to do.

I got certified to teach yoga for the joy of it, with no intention of teaching, and promised myself I would frequently do things for no reason and without a goal.

I turned my energy and attention to writing instead of stealing time out of a hectic day to write.

I have since that moment published a book every six months.

I switched my work from full time employee to a freelancer, a contractor. I didn't realize this at the time but the switch gave me a vantage point — an objectivity, an ability to see things from the outside with a clearer perspective — that vastly increased the value of what I do.

The first year felt like I was establishing something new and now I have more work than I know what to do with.

In the interest of giving the best of me I only work with people whose company I genuinely enjoy.

I recently accepted a full time position and noticed as I run into an office every day my old patterns spring right up: the rushing, the angst, the insomnia, the fear of not knowing what would come next, and allowing my writing to get crowded out.

I flailed, then rearranged things inside of me.

Leaving the corporate world was the best thing I have ever done, not just from a financial perspective but for my soul. If I ever again feel anything is stripping the colors inside of me I will make the same choice again.

Starting Over

And the day came

When the risk to remain

Tight in a bud

Was more painful

Than the risk it took to bloom.

*— **Anais Nin***

Much More Than The Options Available

There is a single life trajectory that is supposed to work for all of us.

Any deviation is cause for anxiety or frowned upon.

College dropout. *When are you getting a job?* You've been dating for a while. *When are you getting married?* You have been married for almost a year. *When are you guys having kids?*

There is not one but an infinite number of ways your life can be glorious and right.

If the one size allegedly fits all path does not work for you this does not mean there is something wrong with you.

Fact: It doesn't work for most of us.

We cannot force our life into a shape that doesn't fit.

Forget what you think "everybody" does. Forget what you are "supposed to do."

Learn to distinguish what you are expected to do from what you really want. This is a necessary discipline for happiness.

From College To The Real World

The transition from college into "the real world" is so frightening.

You feel pressure to figure out who you are and what you want to do for the rest of your life, all while living up to the expectations of the people who love you.

Here is the advice I would have given myself:

Remember this. You will encounter this feeling many times throughout your life. This is your first practice run.

The story that once out of college you "figure things out" and "become an adult" is a lie. You never figure things out, and no one ever becomes an adult.

In our minds, we are all in our teens and twenties wondering how on Earth we became people in our forties.

We are all trying to figure out what it is that we want to do when we grow up and making it up as we go along.

Feeling lost feels discouraging and scary and hopeless, but that's only because we believe we need to "hurry up and get there".

There is no "there".

We need to change the commands in our brain from "hurry up and get there" to "now".

It's all here now.

Instead of feeling small and afraid, regard the possibilities before you as an adventure. You have a chance (many chances) to design your life. Love it now, not at some time in the future.

Before you know it, "now" will become tomorrow.

If you are learning something new, if you are motivated and happy right now, the future will take care of itself.

The answers lie in doing more of what makes you feel fulfilled. But don't ever confuse bliss with an absence of difficulty. Finding your way takes discipline, responsibility, perseverance and sacrifice. Work hard. Commit to something.

Make plans and have goals and write to do lists but leave space for serendipity. Learn how to foster it by keeping an open mind and some free time. Serendipity is a skill essential to happiness. Make room for life to surprise you.

Realize early on that you are going to disappoint the people who love you. You will need to make choices that are true to yourself and often they run counter to what others think you should do.

Hurray for disappointing your parents.

Throughout your life you will find yourself in transitions just as tectonic as leaving college for real life.

The feeling of being lost and needing to start over will be waiting for you at the end of a long relationship you thought was going to last forever.

It will be waiting for you when you decide to have children (or not).

It will be there when you get a divorce, when you face failure, when someone you love dies, when you wake up one morning and realize everything has changed.

When everything is the same and you have changed and nothing fits anymore.

The tools you develop today to thrive within this feeling of being unmoored will serve you for the rest of your life.

Embrace the fact that being lost is part of the human condition.

Questions To Help You Explore What's Next

If life had no meaning, what meaning would I create for mine?

If there was no purpose to our existence, what purpose would I give to mine to shield myself from existential despair?

What matters to me? Why? And once I figure this out, can I determine an order of importance?

Is there a healthy, logical correlation between my priorities and how I spend my time? If not, why?

What am I afraid of? Can I learn to distinguish the fear that protects me from the fear that stops me?

What do I want? Is what I want really what I want or what others have taught me I am supposed to want? How can I tell the difference?

What happens when I get what I want? Is it glorious, empty, triumphant, anticlimactic? Why?

What does happiness mean to me? What makes me happy and how can I capture that elusive sensation more often?

What is my favorite version of myself? When does she show up? How can I get her to stay? *Please. Stay.*

What hurts me? How can I become stronger against what causes me to suffer? How and where can I learn to suffer less? How can I remind myself that the person who makes me suffer the most is me?

Dushka. That could have been so much easier.

What is left of me if I attempt to define myself without leaning on anything I do? I am a student, I am a writer, I am a mom, I am a manager, I am a Vice President — these are all things I do. Who am I? Where is she?

How can I avoid losing myself in my relationships? What are my boundaries and how do I enforce them?

What do my feelings teach me about myself? If I feel anger, or jealousy, can I learn not to react to these feelings but instead determine what they are trying to tell me?

What happens when I sit in silence?

How can I better manage change? How can I get better at accepting how little control I actually have?

How can I always be learning something new?

What would I like to leave behind?

How would I like to be remembered?

Do What You Love

I am a big proponent of *"do what you love"*.

Except that somewhere along the way we forgot the true definition of this sentence. It has become saccharine and vacant; synonymous with an absence of effort.

"Do what you love" does not mean *"only do what gives you pleasure"* or *"you never have to work hard"*.

Doing what you love is less about pleasure and more about being awake.

Wake up.

It's about consciousness, discipline, self-awareness and getting out of your own head to be of service.

It's setting an intention. Committing to something.

It's about hard work.

Doing what you love is doing anything you do with all of you, to the best of your ability, making yourself uncomfortable, doing the right thing even when no one is watching.

There is fire in these things.

How could we ever think that giving up this fire in exchange for instant gratification would ever fulfill us?

This fire is the reason why it's possible to be happy even when you are sad. Because you know you will see this through. Because you will push through it when it hurts.

Because it's difficult and that's not going to stop you.

Because you will meet the calmest, coolest version of yourself in the middle of the toughest situation and discover the joy inherent in grace.

Where To Start

I don't know why it took me so long to realize that humans (and by "humans" I mean me) have a tendency to place the blame for internal shortcomings on outside factors.

Loneliness, for example. I always believed I felt lonely when I lacked someone else's company. Except, sometimes I felt lonely in a room full of people. It stood to reason loneliness was something happening within, not related to anyone else's presence.

It became clear to me that this was the case with cheating too. People who cheat are not necessarily unhappy with their relationships. They are insecure and are looking for confirmation that they are worthy of attention.

It has nothing to do with the love they feel for the people they are with. Nothing.

Or feeling generally misunderstood. If everyone misunderstands me, shouldn't I be explaining myself better?

What if feeling like every single day was the same, was something related to me and not to my job?

I tried to run, of course.

At the end of all that running my realization was that if I didn't deal with things inside me I would take them everywhere and see them replicated over and over.

I had to take a look at how I was approaching the job.

For example:

Trying to get it perfect meant never taking any risks.

It meant the priority was playing it safe, doing only what I already knew how to do. Over and over. (Ah.)

It meant deciding I was bored with it and I could therefore do it while disconnected, like a drone. (Ah.)

It was safer to not care.

I would let my brain switch to "automatic" mode, taking for granted that there was "a way to do things", a "process", instead of considering what it would take to *wake me up.*

What if I tried to do it differently? More creatively? What if I took more risks? What if I saw a routine project as a chance to break that routine?

Because, what if I left my job and took another and within a few months found myself trapped in a labyrinth of identical days, again?

I'm not saying that every job can be a source of enthusiasm and entertainment. I'm not saying that this introspection is easy or even enough.

What I'm saying is that it's the best place to start.

What Do I Do If The 9 To 5 Isn't For Me?

Neither one of my parents ever worked 9:00 to 5:00 so for me that exotic lifestyle only existed in American movies.

When in an unexpected twist of fate I went and got an office job, the routine and structure really suited me: like I had found something I had until then been looking for.

A couple of decades later I felt differently. Like I was trapped. Like someone else got to tell me what to do. Like I was being robbed of what I really wanted to dedicate myself to.

I woke up to the fact that as scary as it sounded I needed to flip my safe life upside down to be excited again by the shape of my days.

Just because something works for "everyone" doesn't mean it works for me. This is an indication that I need to go figure out what does.

Just because something worked for me doesn't mean it always will. This to me is an indication that it's time to reconsider my options.

There are always options.

How To Work Harder

I asked myself what my superpower was (we all have one, you know).

What was it that I loved doing the most?

That thing that I could do all day without getting bored or tired?

What gives me the "where does the time go" feeling?

To answer these questions, I took my time.

Today, I do that for a living.

Don't tell anyone, but it never feels like work.

What Is The Single Most Important Thing To Know About Success?

Success is a story, a narrative, a fabrication. It shifts depending on your (and others) definition of it.

So if you attain "it" or you don't, if you deem yourself a failure or a success, take both those things with a grain of salt.

Neither one is real.

When Was The Last Time You Did Something To Develop Yourself?

It's so easy to get lost in our everyday demands.

Until recently, the most amount of time I ever took off from work was a week.

Then things began to shift. I became increasingly frustrated by things inherent to the work that I do. Things that once seemed like puzzles or interesting challenges began to feel like obstacles, unsurmountable, draining.

I was frequently overwhelmed and felt anxious and frazzled. I was always tired.

I began to feel blue on Sunday afternoons.

One morning, on my way to work, I was looking at email on the bus. I was suddenly gripped by one thought only.

I can't do this anymore.

I knew I desperately needed time to clear my head, to refresh my system, to get inspired.

You know what I felt most of all?

Disconnected from myself.

If you can't remember the last time you did something you develop yourself, I cannot recommend enough that you put something on the calendar.

I'm Rich

Someday I will take serious time off, I'd tell myself. *Someday, when I have enough money saved.*

Alas, my definition of "enough" kept moving out.

I articulated my worst suspicion.

Never. It will never be enough.

If the amount that it will take for me to feel I can take time off keeps moving out and I will never have enough it makes no difference if I take time off now or two years from now or six years from now.

Which can only mean one thing.

I already have enough. I have enough right now.

So I resigned. And every time I have a flare of panic over money, I remind myself I have enough.

My outlook and approach on life when I tell myself I will never have enough and when I tell myself I already have enough changes everything.

The first is anxious, tense, grasping, fearful, despairing. It feels like doom.

The second is relaxed, open, receptive, joyous. It feels like adventure.

They are both equally true so I choose the second.

Evidence that I have enough:

I have time to write (which is to say I have time to do what I love).

I get as much freelance work as I need without feeling like I have to say yes to everything, because I'm not operating from a place of panic.

I loiter or go take a walk in the sun any time I want which in turn inspires me to create. It's also brimming with serendipity and therefore opportunity.

Over the past several weeks, I have overheard friends say they have always wanted something.

"I have always wanted to read Rumi!" one friend said.

"I have been wanting a rain-resistant hat for years now" said another.

I come home and buy whatever they said they wanted and have it shipped to their house.

The ability to buy what someone I love wants confirms to me loud and clear what I have been suspecting for months.

Yeah. I am rich.

Why Is Change So Hard?

"I need you to move from our office in Mexico City to our office in Silicon Valley," said my boss. *"We think you'd be ideal to help run the Apple account."*

This meant one thing. It meant that my life was about to change completely, and I knew it.

The offer to move was fantastic — in the sense of "a fantasy". So fantastic that it was hard to believe. It involved tripling my salary, moving from Mexico City to California, and working on an iconic brand for a company I loved.

It also meant giving my nascent long distance relationship a real shot.

It was as if I had wished for a thousand implausible wishes and angels had descended from heaven to grant them all at the same time.

I should have been ecstatic. And I was.

Except also I wasn't.

Change arrives with contradictory feelings. I was happy/sad, scared/amazed, grateful/no, no please I can't do this but thank you for thinking of me go away.

It implied taking every single thing I knew and that was important to me, including my country, my home, my family, my friends, a job I was doing well at — and chucking it and starting over in a new country where I had nothing and knew no one.

Who does that? This is crazy.

This is thrilling/terrifying.

I have to.

As I packed everything I owned and gave most of it away and celebrated and said goodbye and was congratulated and cheered on I hid from myself that I was massively sad.

I was supposed to feel privileged and honored and blessed but I was mourning.

I didn't want to seem ungrateful to all those angels but truth be told I was giving up a lot.

This is the crux of the matter. Change is loss, even when it's gain.

And, the way things actually are is often at odds with the way things are supposed to be.

This is what I tell myself now: to make change easier forget everything about how things are supposed to be. It's OK to feel free when you think you should be devastated. It's OK to mourn when you're supposed to be celebrating.

It's OK to feel terrified when everyone thinks you can do it except for you. Or when you are sure you can and nobody believes you.

It's OK to sometimes not even like the people you are supposed to love, or to be attracted to others when you're supposed to have eyes for only one person.

All of these things are OK because they are real and true and this is life.

It's OK to stand at the edge of a metaphorical cliff and look down and think "this is insane" when you know you have to take that leap.

It's OK to really, really not want to.

Practice

Practice is revolutionary.

It is the most underestimated, most powerful tool available to us.

It's the door to understanding something. To learning something. To getting good at something. To getting better at something.

It's the way to accomplish something I never thought I could.

It's how something I previously thought impossible one day becomes easy.

But most of all, practice is where you meet yourself.

Let's say I want to become a good writer. What will it take?

Practice. To be a good writer, I need to write.

Let's say I'm going to practice from Monday to Sunday, every day.

If I start on Monday, will I be slightly better by Friday?

Not necessarily.

Monday might be rusty. Tuesday might be smoother. Wednesday, catastrophic. Thursday I want to give up and never practice again.

This isn't working. Why did I think this was a good idea?

Friday is frustrating and difficult.

Saturday is smooth.

Sunday is —

What a waste.

The lesson here is not in getting better or worse but in how I meet my bad days and my good days.

Do I get exasperated? Do I give up? Do I run?

I want to run.

Can I learn to meet my bad days with equanimity, to have bad days not matter so that my emotions remain stable while my skill does what it will?

Practice cannot be about right or wrong.

It's about showing up, accepting where I am at and realizing that if I consider it similar to repetition, if I consider it tedious, I am missing the point.

It's a gift: something I can count on forever.

It will always be there waiting for me.

Even if I get everything wrong a thousand times I can always, always begin again.

First Thing To Do After You Fail

Failure implies that there has been a fight, a struggle, a ferocious swimming against the current.

It means things did not go the way I expected.

It means I feel defeated, deflated, inadequate and probably depleted.

My first course of action would be to turn off my phone, push everything aside and nap.

I can go for a run later, make calls later, work on my resume later, clean the house and restore order inside of me later.

First, a nap.

Nothing distorts the way you see things like exhaustion.

Rest heals. It tells my body that despite the recent catastrophe I am safe. It puts everything in perspective.

Perspective is what I need the most.

Set it all down and nap.

What Is The Difference Between A Habit And A Ritual?

A habit is an activity you have repeated so many times that your brain switches to automatic. You don't have to think. You don't do it because you want to. You don't even question it.

Our life is a system of habits that are all interconnected. Changing one can (and often does) affect the others.

Changing your habits is a certain way to change your life but it's hard to do because most of them have faded into the fabric of your days and have become invisible. You can't change what you can't see.

A ritual is the opposite of a habit. It requires your full presence and attention and as such it wakes up your brain.

There is something sacred in a ritual. Its meaning is bigger than the immediate action you are taking. Connection. Community. Awareness. Devotion.

Why Do We Keep Making The Same Mistakes?

Imagine a jungle, verdant, lush, thick with vegetation.

You come along with a machete and painstakingly, laboriously clear a path to walk on.

You use it every day, back and forth, and slowly realize this path of yours, while well trodden, is not ideal.

If you had known then what you know now you might have chosen a flatter, easier route, one with a better view, less fraught with risk.

You realize this, but know an alternate path does not currently exist.

You would have to grab that machete and begin again the arduous work of clearing a new way.

This takes monumental effort. Not just because it's difficult but because it feels counterintuitive.

Better to use the existing path, despite the evidence that another could be better.

When you do things a certain way — habits, routines, beliefs, proclivities, assumptions — you are in effect carving out a neural pathway in your brain.

Repetition makes it wider, more comfortable.

Creating a new path doesn't feel natural — it doesn't even feel possible — and as such you default again and again into the one you know.

It's who I am, you say. *The cross I have to bear. The cards I was dealt.*

It's my destiny.

This is why habits are hard to break, why we fall into patterns we know make us suffer but can't seem to redesign.

But we can.

There is even a name for it: neuroplasticity.

We can determine what it is we want to build. We can do this if we remind ourselves how making the same mistake over and over is hurting us.

We can envision what a better way might look like if we decided once and for all to embrace the fact that if you are willing to put in the work there is always a better way.

Just because you believe you can't get there from here doesn't make it true.

The clearing of this new path would go slowly at first. We'd often be working in darkness, in the absence of faith, burdened by fatigue, sorrow or despair.

One day soon this new path, once unfathomable, unattainable, unimaginable, will be obvious, easy, wide and sunny.

This is how it's always possible to clear space for future behavior, better patterns, more intentional, more purposeful habits.

This is how we can set ourselves up to finally arrive at a better outcome.

I Loiter And Loaf

One of my most agonizing, most visceral fears was going from a full time employee to unemployed.

The notion of completely empty days with nothing to fill them petrified me.

This terror kept me shackled to a way of life that made me feel both safe and suffocated.

Is "safe" worth it if it traps you?

One day I decided it was time to turn decades of a very structured life on its head. It was time to follow my own advice and do what I was most afraid of.

I quit my job and, well. I don't know how else to put this: I adapted instantly.

To my utter shock, I have a natural inclination towards loitering.

I loaf. I lounge. I linger. I dawdle.

I know. This does not sound particularly dashing. My admission does not exactly portray a hero's journey.

Still, I consider this my greatest success and as such challenge the notion that to succeed I have to suffer.

Don't Work For Free

The rhythm of my work varies. I am often completely booked and having to turn down clients. Other times, less often, I have time available.

How could I put this time to the best use?

I realized one day that there were many organizations out there doing important work who could not afford to hire me. What I do is expensive, and offering someone guidance on how to communicate better would be a clear way for me to contribute to their cause.

To organizations doing work I considered valuable I would offer my services for free.

What an excellent idea.

My beloved, incredibly business savvy friend Christopher Lochhead saw me making this offer through my social media channels and messaged me immediately. *"Dushka! Never work for free! What a terrible idea!"* he said.

I was grateful for the fact he looks after me but I didn't listen, mostly because my brain tends to brush advice aside. This is unfortunate, because if I heeded advice I'd save so much time.

Regrettably, I need to figure things out on my own.

Whenever I offered my work for free, things fell through. Organizations were excited and thanked me profusely, after which they would not follow up. They would block time on my calendar and then cancel at the last minute.

After I realized this was a pattern more than a series of unfortunate coincidences, I saw clearly that Christopher had been right.

People do not take seriously what they don't pay for.

I don't do pro bono work anymore, and I make no exceptions.

My Five Year Plan

Today I will go to a long yoga class. I will try many different poses I know I can't do, just to not shy away from difficulty, effort or incompetence.

Just to remind myself perfection is not worth my time.

Today I will try to be considerate of others. Put myself in another person's shoes.

I will be generous. For example, I will assume everyone is doing the best they can.

I will pick the healthiest option on the menu rather than the most crispy.

I will read instead of watching TV and write rather than let myself get distracted by all the things I'm so very easily distracted by.

I will assume responsibility.

I will do my best work.

I will spend time with people who matter to me. For example, I'm going to call my mom.

I will give something away, preferably something I really like, as a reminder that I have enough.

I will replace all the voices in my head that tell me I am in danger with voices that remind me that so far I've been pretty stellar at taking care of myself.

I'll tell fear to go away.

I will trust the people that I love.

I will celebrate uncertainty.

I will bow deeply to beautiful things I don't believe in.

I will go to bed early because I could always use an extra hour of sleep.

I will do all these things and bet you anything that if I keep it up the next five years will take care of themselves.

Who Wins At Life?

I hope you are making a lot of mistakes.

I hope you get your heart broken.

You can't win at life without losing so I hope you are open to losing a lot.

I hope that you remain a beginner forever.

That you are a participant.

That you are creating something and that it gnaws at you. That you sacrifice time with friends to make space for your creation.

I hope that you are always learning.

That you feel you are running out of time.

That you overextend yourself. Bite off more than you can chew.

That you are never in a hurry. (Yes, of course this is a contradiction. This is real life.)

I hope you are part of a community.

That you know you can't afford to criticize someone, in particular someone you don't know.

I hope you see the beauty that is in everything.

I hope that you feel lost sometimes.

That you enjoy your own company.

That you are the one who loves more.

That both trusting and forgiving come easy.

That your yeses are abundant and frequent and your nos unequivocal.

That you are never far away from nature.

That you can see competition is a fallacy and that you are enough.

That you shun fighting and drama and know how to stand up for yourself.

I hope that you can always open a window.

I wish all these things for you because I know no other way to win at life than this.

Shooting Star

You are not static.

Regardless of your age everything inside you is roiling. We tend to perceive ourselves as rocks or trees, rooted. We are more like fire, like shooting stars in a wide, sparkling trajectory of light.

Everything around you is changing too.

We are unstable sailors trying to keep our footing as we stand on rocky boats.

This means that to subsist we need to constantly recalibrate.

The next time you declare you are lost, think about this. You are not lost. You are finding yourself.

The next time you feel alone realize that this is just sensation, an irrational impossibility if you have yourself.

The next time you feel inadequate consider that instead you are learning. You are a student.

And if you are able to regard yourself and realize it was you, your fault, that you were responsible for what happened, then you are also a teacher.

I guarantee you will come back from this. It will be better precisely because of what you are now learning.

You will be found again, feel connected again, feel useful again.

I also absolutely guarantee future disorientation, confusion, isolation and desolation.

I guarantee you will again fear you will never work again. You will wonder why you keep making the same mistakes.

At these times, do not despair. Go to the mirror and remind yourself.

I am not lost. I am finding myself. I am not alone — I have me.

I am already perfect, in a state of necessary, natural recalibration.

Perfect, and forever a work in progress.

I am a shooting star.

Made in the USA
Columbia, SC
22 June 2021